THE
PHALLACY
OF
GENESIS

LITERARY
CURRENTS
IN
BIBLICAL
INTERPRETATION

THE
PHALLACY
OF
GENESIS

---

a feminist-
psychoanalytic
approach

ILONA N. RASHKOW

•

WESTMINSTER/JOHN KNOX PRESS
Louisville, Kentucky

THE PHALLACY OF GENESIS:
A FEMINIST-PSYCHOANALYTIC APPROACH

First edition

Published by Westminster/John Knox Press,
Louisville, Kentucky

This book is printed on acid-free paper that meets the American National Standards Institute Z39.48 standard. ∞

PRINTED IN THE UNITED STATES OF AMERICA
2 4 6 8 9 7 5 3 1

Library of Congress Cataloging-in-Publication Data

Rashkow, Ilona N. (Ilona Nemesnyik)
    The phallacy of Genesis : a feminist-psychoanalytic approach / Ilona N. Rashkow. — 1st ed.
        p.   cm. — (Literary currents in biblical interpretation)
    Includes bibliographical references and indexes.
    ISBN 0-664-25250-8 (pbk. : alk. paper)

    1. Bible. O.T. Genesis—Criticism, interpretation, etc. 2. Bible. O.T. Genesis—Psychology. 3. Psychoanalysis and religion. 4. Bible as literature. 5. Psychoanalysis and literature. 6. Feminist literary criticism. I. Title. II. Series.
BS1235.2.R38 1993
222'.1106—dc20
                                                            93-19548

אֲנִי לְדוֹדִי וְדוֹדִי לִי

To Bruce

ACKNOWLEDGMENTS

Parts of chapter 4 appear in a different form in *The New Literary Criticism and the Hebrew Bible*, ed. J. Cheryl Exum and David J. A. Clines (Sheffield: JSOT Press, 1993). Reprinted by permission of Sheffield Academic Press, Ltd.

Parts of chapter 2 appear in a different form in *Reading Between Texts: Intertextuality and the Hebrew Bible*, ed. Danna Nolan Fewell (Louisville: Westminster/John Knox Press, 1992). Reprinted by permission of Westminster/John Knox Press.

Quotation from the poem by R. D. Laing in chapter 2 is from *Knots*, by R. D. Laing (Harmondworth: Penguin, 1974). Reprinted by permission of Travistock Publications.

Words were originally magic and to this day words have retained much of their ancient magical power. By words one person can make another blissfully happy or drive him to despair, by words the teacher conveys his knowledge to his pupils, by words the orator carries his audience with him and determines their judgements and decisions. Words provoke affects and are in general the means of mutual influence among men.

—Sigmund Freud (1926e:183)

Ishkabibble-fribble.

—Tyler Fairbanks Warden[1]

CONTENTS

SERIES
PREFACE

New currents in biblical interpretation are emerging. Questions about origins—authors, intentions, settings—and stages of composition are giving way to questions about the literary qualities of the Bible, the play of its language, the coherence of its final form, and the relations between text and readers.

Such literary criticism is rapidly acquiring sophistication as it learns from major developments in secular critical theory, especially in understanding the instability of language and the key role of readers in the production of meaning. Biblical critics are being called to recognize that a plurality of readings is an inevitable and legitimate consequence of the interpretive process. By the same token, interpreters are being challenged to take responsibility for the theological, social, and ethical implications of their readings.

Biblical interpretation is changing on the practical as well as the theoretical level. More readers, both inside and outside the academic guild, are discovering that the Bible in literary perspective can powerfully engage people's lives. Communities of faith where the Bible is foundational may find that literary criticism can make the Scripture accessible in a way that historical criticism seems unable to do.

Within these changes lie exciting opportunities for all who seek contemporary meaning in the ancient texts. The goal of the series is to encourage such change and such search, to breach the confines of traditional biblical criticism, and to open channels for new currents of interpretation.

—THE EDITORS

PREFACE

Translations of biblical passages are my own, in consultation with the major modern Bible translations.

This book is the product of several years of research, writing, and introspection, and I am grateful to many for their help during this period.

The State University of New York at Stony Brook has been my professional home and I appreciate the suggestions given by my colleagues, particularly Louise Vasvari, Sandy Petrey, Krin Gabbard, and Sue Bottigheimer. I also thank the Meyerhoff Center of Jewish Studies for inviting me to be a visiting research fellow and allowing me to share my ideas.

In the course of my research I have benefitted from the expertise of others whom I acknowledge here with pleasure and gratitude. Adele Berlin has enriched my understanding of the Hebrew Bible and of literature in general. She is an inspiration and a friend. This book owes its actual existence in great part to Jesse Rubin whose insight, encouragement, and enthusiasm have kept me going. I also thank David Gunn, Danna Nolan Fewell, and Tim Beal for their apt comments and help throughout this project.

I thank my parents, Helen and John Nemesnyik, for standing by me throughout this long, sometimes difficult process and for demonstrating, by surviving the writing of this book, the strength of parental love.

None of this would have been possible, however, without my husband Bruce, the best reader I know. He listened to my theories, gave me support and encouragement, lightened my discouragements, and helped me with all my revisions. Bruce is and remains my beloved. I affectionately dedicate this book to him.

1

READING
(ABOUT)
THIS
READING

Much [of this text] contradicts traditional opinions and
wounds deeply-rooted feelings . . . it is bound . . . to provoke.
—Sigmund Freud (1916-17:11)

THE BIBLE AND PSYCHOANALYTIC LITERARY THEORY

If the "strength" of literature can be defined by the intensity of
its impact on readers, the Hebrew Bible would doubtless qualify
as one of the "strongest" (that is, most effective) texts of all
time. Simply judging by the quantity and intensity of commentaries it has produced, few literary texts have provoked so many
interpretations, so many exegetic passions, and so many ener-
getic controversies.

Until recently, reading the Bible was thought to be a rather
straightforward procedure. The goal was to respond "properly"
by trying to "understand" the text and grasp the "meaning."
The unspoken and unwritten rule was: "Do not confuse what
you are doing to the text with what it is doing to you. The
proper aim of biblical exegesis is the apprehension of the text
itself."

In spite of the impressive pressures designed to preserve this
view of reading Scripture (within both the academy and society
at large), the rules seemed to change when the Bible became an
object of interest to literary theorists. Post-structural literary

criticism was particularly forceful in calling attention to the problematic interaction between reader and text. Scholars were producing counterexamples of irreducibly different and often contradictory readings of the same biblical narratives, and the wealth of interpretations had the effect of undermining the long-established and accepted doctrine of "objectivity." "Reader-oriented" or "reader-response" criticism soon gained wide acceptance within biblical studies. As David Clines observes, "What has happened . . . in the last three decades can be represented . . . as a shift in focus that has moved from *author* to *text* to *reader*" (1990:9-10); readers "*use* the Bible today . . . in terms of *their values, attitudes, and responses*" (McKnight 1988:14-15, emphasis added). In other words, *how* the biblical text is read is determined, in great part, by *who* does the reading.

This application of literary criticism to biblical scholarship inevitably brings together different methodologies, one of which applies the principles of psychology to the reading of the Bible. While the realms of psychology and reading seem quite disparate, in fact the interplay of literature and psychology dates back to antiquity. Although Aristotle did not use psychoanalytic terms, he did speak of aesthetic experience as inspired "frenzy" or "emotional catharsis." The formal coupling of literature and psychoanalysis goes back to Freud himself, who concluded his famous essay "Creative Writers and Day-Dreaming" (1908e) with the suggestion that artistic works allow the audience to revel in their own forbidden fantasies. It would appear, based on the statements of Clines, McKnight, and Freud, that many of us, wittingly or otherwise, have been producing psychoanalytic readings of biblical narratives!

But what makes a reading of a literary work "psychoanalytic?" To call a reading "psychoanalytic" or "Freudian" immediately introduces ambiguity, because such an expression can refer either to the use of Freudian themes or to Freudian methods. That is, an interpretation of a literary work can be called "Freudian" or "psychoanalytic" with respect either to the substance of the text, the meaning or thematic content it derives from a narrative (in other words, *what* it reads), or to the interpretive procedures and techniques a reader uses (*how* it reads).

Until recently, most psychoanalytic approaches to literature[1] have centered on an analysis of personal psyche, whether that of the writer or the literary character. Indeed, there is a long tradition of Freudian criticism that seeks the literary work for the buried motives and "hidden neurotic conflicts" that generate a writer's art. We are all familiar with the texts psychoanalysts have used as "evidence" of the unconscious intentionality of their authors. In writing *Hamlet*, for example, Shakespeare was working over the death of his son (Jones 1949); and in writing *The Gambler* Dostoevski was drawing upon the prohibitions placed upon masturbation in his childhood (Freud 1928b). But psychoanalyzing a writer is speculative business and runs into the same problems which David Gunn describes when trying to determine authorial intent:

> The problems that arise in talking of the author's intention (in connection with much Old Testament material) are not dissimilar to those which confront the critic who demands a precise knowledge of the story's original social context as the key to its exegesis, given the paucity of extant socio-historical data from ancient Israel and the problems of dating and identifying the author(s) and editor(s) of particular texts. (1980:136, n. 6)

In all three cases—psychoanalyzing the writer, determining authorial intent, and establishing a narrative's historical context—the hazards are inversely proportional to the amount of material available on the writer's life and private thoughts. It is never completely safe to guess at the "psychic significance" of a piece of literature to the author of the work, even that of a candid living author. For biblical writers, we have only the most minimal sense of what their private lives may have been like. Further, some of the less scrupulous exponents have given this type of psychoanalytic literary criticism a bad name (a cigar, as Freud said, is sometimes just a cigar).[2]

A more popular mode of criticism is to focus not on the author but on the literary characters. Freud's own ventures into literature were along this line. His initial remarks on the Oedipus complex were literary, involving both Hamlet and Oedipus

Tyrannis. Hamlet, thus read, is "the hysteric" who delays because he is paralyzed by guilt over Claudius' enactment of his own unconscious wishes (1916-17:335). From this brief remark sprang Ernest Jones's elaborations on Hamlet and Oedipus (1949). A stream of essays by other analysts followed, mostly on fictitious textual characters. They wrote what might be described as "case studies" of literature, dealing with those authors or characters whom they categorized as "neurotic." Most of them emphasized such analytic themes as the Oedipus complex, anality, schizoid tendencies, latent or expressed homosexuality, guilt, etc., and the roles they played in the works of the writers or among their other literary characters.[3]

This approach has not fallen into as deep a disrepute as concentrating on the writer, in great part because fictional characters are viewed as representatives of life and as such can be understood only if we assume that they are "telling a truth." This assumption allows us to find "unconscious" motivations, albeit in fictitious characters. For example, Abraham's actions and language reveal a great deal about him, despite the fact that all we will ever "know" is contained in the 1,534 verses of Genesis.

On the other hand, biblical characters are both more and less than real persons. This presents a problem. While one aspect of narrative characterization is to provide a *mimetic* function, that is, to represent human action and motivation, another aspect is primarily *textual*, that is, to reveal information to a reader or to conceal it. This situation has no precise parallel in life (although it can be argued that real persons often resemble literary characters in the masks they present to the world). As a result, examining a narrative character is not risk-free either. For instance, contradictions in Abraham's character may result from the psychic complexities the biblical writer imagined; on the other hand, they may result from the fact that Abraham is an agent in a literary narrative with a highly developed system of conventions.[4] That is, his "traits" may be more a function of the requirements of the story-line than his personality. In other words, if we cannot even ask "How many children had Lady Macbeth?" as Norman Holland warns (1964), then we certainly cannot determine the extent or even the existence of Abraham's neuroses.

THE ROLE OF THE READER

More recently, character analysis has challenged assumptions about the *nature* of literary characterization. Interest in the unconscious existence of literary characters has led to questions about just where "character" or the "self" is located, especially as the interrelations of literature and other fields such as philosophy, anthropology, and sociology have been explored. As a result, the literary character's distinction from his or her role and his or her world is no longer as clear as it once was. That is, since literature contributes to our imaginings of personal experience, literary characters carry their "psychology" within themselves, in the very structure of relations they embody, and invite us to form with them as readers. Thus, in some way (however obscure), the literary work contains its origins and significance as a "psychologically coherent act" (Schwartz and Willbern 1982:205), despite its fictive nature. As readers, we seek to experience and understand the literary character's role and world, even though we acknowledge the narrative as fictitious.

In psychoanalytic literary theory, this change in approach focuses on the "way" the reader and a text work together, and is based on the theory that the unconscious is structured like a language. Rather than seeing the literary text as a "case history," it can be treated much like the raw materials of an actual "analysis"—the succession of stories, occasional lyric, autobiography, and discursive monologues which make up free association. From this perspective, a reader imitates a psychoanalyst by looking beyond the literal story to relate its structure and conflicts to a drama within some *theoretical* human mind, a mind ambiguously located between the fictional characters of the text and that of the reader. It is primarily in this area that reader-oriented criticism makes literary use of the psychoanalytic process.

One of the earliest theorists to use this "reader-oriented" method of literary criticism was Louise Rosenblatt, whose work in 1938 pioneered the notion of reading as a *transaction* between text and reader:

> Through the medium of words, the text brings into the reader's consciousness certain concepts, certain sensuous experiences, certain images of things, people, actions, and scenes. The special meanings and, more particularly, the submerged associations that the words and images have for the individual reader will largely determine what the work communicates to *him*. The reader brings to the work personality traits, memories of past events, present needs and preoccupations, a particular mood of the moment, and a particular physical condition. These and many other elements in a never-to-be-duplicated combination determine his response to the peculiar contribution of the text. (1938:30-31)[5]

Of course, reader-oriented criticism is no more a conceptually unified critical position in biblical studies than in literary studies generally. It is a term that has come to be associated with scholars who use "reader," "the reading process," and "response" as areas for investigation. Indeed, there are several different varieties of reader-response criticism (such as rhetorical, semiotic, phenomenological, sociological, historical, feminist, psychoanalytic, etc.). To make matters even more confusing, these approaches are neither monolithic (there is more than one *kind* of rhetorical, semiotic, phenomenological, sociological, historical, feminist, psychoanalytic, etc. criticism). Nor do they mutually exclude each other (a critic may use more than one approach, even in the same reading). Indeed, the vitality of reader-response criticism depends precisely on the notion that various dimensions of exegesis or interpretation are possible, and that a combination of approaches is not negative dilettantism but positive eclecticism.

Despite different methodologies, what can be said with some measure of assurance is that all reader-oriented biblical criticism focuses on both the Bible *and* the reader, be it the biblical authors' attitudes towards the ancient readers, the kinds of readers various texts seem to imply,[6] the role actual readers play in the determination of literary meaning, the relation of reading strategies to textual interpretation, the status of the reader's "self," or something else. The "objectivity" of the text and of the reading process are concepts which, intended or not, reader-oriented biblical criticism inevitably opposes. For instance, if readers find anal imagery in the characterization of Moses, are they revealing the biblical writer's fixations or only their own?[7] Most reader-response critics would argue that since a narrative has no meaning before it is read, there can be no distinction between what is "in" a narrative and what is "in" a reader. Hence, neither a text nor a reader can be "objective."

Among non-biblical literary theorists, this opposition ranges from timid qualifications of the doctrine of textual autonomy to frontal assaults on the idea of objectivity itself. As an example, Wolfgang Iser and Michael Riffaterre make statements such as "the reader's enjoyment begins when he himself becomes productive" (Iser 1978:108) and the "semiotic process really takes place in the reader's mind" (Riffaterre 1978:4). Walter Slatoff reduces the importance of the text even further: "works of literature have scarcely any important qualities apart from those that take shape in our minds" (1970:23). Reader-oriented critics influenced by structuralism not only deny that literary texts have meaning in and of themselves, but also that individual readers can create their own meanings. Thus, Jonathan Culler writes, "The poem . . . has meaning only with respect to a system of conventions which the reader has assimilated" (1975:116), and Stanley Fish declares, "The objectivity of the text is an allusion . . . there are no fixed texts but only interpretive strategies making them" (1980:170; 1980a:90).

Reader-oriented biblical scholars seem to agree that "meaning" does not inhere completely and exclusively in the text. The "effects" of reading Scripture, psychological and otherwise, are essential to its "meaning" since "meaning" has no existence outside the mind of a reader. This seems to be borne out by the fact that each time we read a biblical narrative we see something new, not because biblical interpretation is inexhaustible but because each time we read a text we are at least slightly different people having experienced more of life's vicissitudes.

Ultimately, what this process of reader-oriented literary criticism yields in biblical studies is not an approach based *solely* on the concept of the reader, but a way of looking at biblical narratives *and* readers which reorganizes both their interrelationships and the distinctions between them. To quote Jane Tompkins, "Reading and writing join hands, change places, and finally become distinguishable only as two names for the same activity" (1980a:x). Recognizing the relationship of a reader to a text leads to a more profound awareness that no one biblical interpretation is intrinsically "true." Meaning does not stand waiting to be uncovered behind a text, but evolves in front of it, actualized by readers and interpreters who produce new possibilities. Thus, biblical exegetes, like all readers, are in fact caught up in the very narratives we wish to explicate and play an interpretive role in the story.

As a result, the principle that readings vary with new historical situations is extended to the point where it is completely transformed. While previously it was assumed that new readings could produce only small variations in a relatively fixed canon of ideas, the concept that readers "make readings" diminishes the number of fixed, or relatively fixed, meanings and vastly increases the possibilities of new interpretations. Indeed, under this approach the number of novel explications becomes endless.

READING THE BIBLE AND THE PSYCHOANALYTIC PROCESS: SOME PARALLELS

Since the role of an individual reader is the essence of this work, it is necessary to say a few words about some of the parallels I see between reading Scripture and the psychoanalytic process. Indeed, I see reading as a replication of the psychoanalytic process itself. Thus, this book is a reading *of* reading. Let me explain.

In some cases the parallels between the psychoanalytic process and reading the biblical text are easy to see. Shifts in meaning of individual words and phrases are important to both psychoanalysts and readers. The more recent definition of the psychoanalytic process as a "switching between two ways of seeing" (Skura 1981:218) corresponds to one of the most traditional aspects of literary criticism in at least three ways.

First, on the level of individual words and phrases, shifts have been studied as ambiguities of various kinds and are the necessary wealth of alternatives which make "poetic" language and language poetic.

Second, in broader, if vaguer, forms, they have been studied as the "irony" which makes biblical narratives so appealing.[8]

Third, on a larger scale, the plot movement of tragedy described by Aristotle resembles stylized psychoanalysis or at least what Meredith Skura describes as the "old-style traumatic revelation analysis" (1981:224). In both cases, there is a recognition not only of a *specific* fact but of a fact which changes everything, making us give up one set of values and the belief that the world conforms to them. (Not surprisingly, nearly all the narratives I discuss have this kind of plot.) As a result, the reorganization of the role of a reader and a reader's relationship to a text affects something more fundamental than the experience of the character in the narrative or the plot alone: it touches the reader's *unconscious* and produces an effect on the reader's *self*-consciousness. In other words, if biblical characters such as Abraham sometimes suffer from clichés, as a reader, so do I.

A second parallel between reading and psychoanalysis is that reading, like the psychoanalytic process, begins with the assumption that communication has many facets. Therefore, both a reader and a psychoanalyst must draw on "all the ways by which one human being understands another" (Loewenstein 1957:132). Just as a psychoanalyst is as interested in why and how something is said as in the words that are actually being spoken, so a reader tries to be open to sudden changes and word displacements in a text. In both reading and psychoanalysis, there is an editorial "openness" and a suspension of all conclusions.

By incorporating both *what* a text says and *how* a text says it, reading and psychoanalysis emphasize moments of insight and *self*-consciousness. Reading, like psychoanalysis, diverts, displaces, and elaborates upon meanings, expanding images into webs of associations or condensing a flow of statements into a single focusing insight. By shifting meanings and perspectives, "rules" for the interpretations of "texts" change.

That everyone responds to the Hebrew Bible in his or her own way is not noteworthy in itself. But since Aristotle, we have suspected that underlying our various responses there are principles to be described. Although Aristotle did not use the psychoanalytic term "identification," he did speak of imitation and sympathy. Thus, another parallel I see between reading and the psychoanalytic process is a certain suspension of critical will, which opens one to change, the kind of change which breaks old schemata or the way we see them, and ultimately the way we see the world. It is for this reason that applying the psychoanalytic process to biblical texts seems most natural. The Hebrew Bible is a religious text and, as such, it is reasonable for a reader to assume it illustrates moral principles. As readers, we want and expect this text to reflect the kind of world with which we know how to deal.

To tie this concept back to Aristotle, reading results in the particular therapeutic effect he calls "catharsis":

> An emotion which strongly affects some souls is present in all to a varying degree, for example pity and fear, and also ecstasy. To this last some people are particularly liable, and we see that under the influence of religious music and songs which drive the soul to frenzy, they calm down as if they had been medically treated and purged. People who are given to pity and fear, and emotional people generally, and others to the extent that they have similar emotions, must be affected in the same way; for all of them must experience a kind of purgation [catharsis] and pleasurable relief. (Grube 1958:xv-xvi)

If Aristotle is correct, the reason a reader experiences "pleasurable relief" is because he or she "identifies" with the narrative character, a term introduced into literary criticism by Percy Bysshe Shelley, who elegantly expresses the "modern" common-sense attitude toward the hero:

> Homer embodies the ideal perfection of his age in human character; nor can we doubt that those who read his verse were awakened to an ambition of *becoming like to Achilles,*

Hector, and Ulysses: . . . the sentiments of the auditors must have been refined and enlarged by a sympathy with such great and lovely impersonations, until from admiring they imitated, and from imitation they identified themselves with the objects of their admiration. Nor let it be objected that these characters are remote from moral perfection, and that they can by no means be considered as edifying patterns for general imitation. (1821:430, emphasis added)

But to quote Hamlet, "Ay, there's the rub." It is difficult to imagine a reader with "an ambition of becoming like to Achilles," much less wanting to shoulder Moses's responsibilities.

We identify with biblical characters, of course; but Freud, extending Shelley's thoughts, teaches us that there are forms of identification which do not stem from admiration and imitation. For example, Abraham, a figure of towering proportions and often terrifying features, whose character is idiosyncratic and flawed, is an ideal with which we can identify only indirectly or in a highly specialized sense. And our identification is complicated by unconscious factors. For instance, the way Abraham deals with Abimelech may inspire guilt in us and we might react defensively.

But the powerful effect of biblical narratives on readers may be explained also in other than moral terms. Fish and his concept of "community of like-minded readers" (1980) notwithstanding, there is little agreement about the moral principles operating in much of the Bible; and it is not improbable that an ancient reader had as difficult a time as a modern one understanding the narrative account of the deity "hardening Pharaoh's heart" and then sending the plagues. Both might ask, "Did Pharaoh *really* deserve that?" Inevitably, our reaction to these narratives is psychological. That is, in reading the Hebrew Bible, we try to shape the text until it is the kind of setting in which we can gratify our wishes and defeat our fears. A fourth parallel.

2

INTERTEXTUALITY
AND TRANSFERENCE:
A READER IN/OF
GENESIS 12:10-20
AND 20:1-18

Since Jack is afraid
that Jill will think that
Jack is afraid
Jack pretends that Jack is not afraid of Jill
so that Jill will be more afraid of Jack.

—R. D. Laing, *Knots*

This chapter focuses on the relationship between the literary text and reader in the context of the psychoanalytic concept of "transference."[1] Transference is generally considered to be the very essence of Freudian theory. Briefly described, in the course of treatment the analysand (or patient) may unconsciously "transfer" on to the analyst (or doctor) the conflicts he or she is experiencing. If a patient has a difficult time dealing with his or her father, for example, he or she may unconsciously cast the analyst in that parental role. As a result, the analyst has particular insight into the analysand's psychical life and can "trigger" responses in the analysand. In this chapter, I discuss how a literary text, similar to an analyst, "triggers" responses in a reader.

Simultaneously, this chapter explores how a text influences a reader to conduct a *self*-analysis, to examine his or her own responses to a narrative. My thesis is two-fold: first, a reader acts as both analyst *and* analysand; and second, the relation of text and reader is in constant exchange.

This interaction between reader and text occurs, in part, because of what literary theorists call "intertextuality," the relation of a particular text to other texts. According to this theory, a work can be read only in connection with or against other texts. As Iser writes:

> Whatever we have read sinks into our memory and is fore-shortened. It may later be evoked again and set against a different background with the result that the reader is enabled to develop hitherto unforeseeable connections. . . . Thus *the reader*, in establishing these interrelations between past, present, and future, actually *causes the text to reveal its potential multiplicity of connections.* (1974:125, emphasis added)

In other words, a reader acts as an analyst who points out "slips" in the text. Due to intertextuality, the text acts as a reader's analyst as well by enabling a reader to draw certain analogies and conclusions.

As elaborated upon below, within the psychoanalytic framework, by virtue of transference, the analysand tries to force or coax the analyst to "play out a scene" he or she remembers, though the analysand is not aware of either the coaxing or the scene as such (Freud 1912b:97-108). Just as the psychoanalytic concept of transference is a structure of repetition linking analyst and analysand, literary intertextuality is a repetition of the very structure it seeks to understand. In both the reading process and the psychoanalytic process, a new, more complete narrative is ultimately generated.

The biblical focus of this chapter is the literary topos dealing with the "Matriarch of Israel in Danger." In three places in Genesis, different combinations of patriarchs, matriarchs, foreign kings, and social settings are recorded, but the scenario and key terms basically coincide. All three passages give essentially the same story: a patriarch and his wife visit a foreign land. Fearing that the woman's beauty might become a source of danger to himself as the husband, the man resorts to subterfuge by claiming that his wife is his sister. In Genesis 12, the encounter involves Abraham and Sarah with the ruler of Egypt. The incident is repeated twice: in Genesis 20 the same couple confronts Abimelech of Gerar; and in Genesis 26 Abimelech is similarly embarrassed by Isaac and Rebekah. Although there are three patriarch/wife/other occurrences in Genesis, this chapter uses only the Abraham/Sarah cycle (Genesis 12 and 20) as a paradigm for reading intertextually.

THE RELATIONSHIP OF GENESIS 12, 20, AND 26 ACCORDING TO "SOURCE" CRITICISM

Since the nineteenth-century studies by Wellhausen, biblical scholarship has tended to assign the "authorship" of biblical narratives to four major sources: "J," or Yahwist, for its use of the divine name YHWH; "E," or Elohist, for its use of the divine name Elohim; "D," or Deuteronomist, understood as the source of Deuteronomy and editor of Joshua through Kings; and "P," or Priestly writer, source of the cultic laws of the Torah and material of a genealogical and archival nature. These categories have, in recent years, come under question because, for one, the separation into sources does little to explain the larger unities that exist in biblical narrative. Some such criticisms have been allayed by speaking of a biblical "redactor," who merged the various alleged "sources" into their present arrangement.

Source critics have studied "textual duplications," accumulating knowledge about similar narratives, and categorizing events or motifs which occur more than once in the same story or story cycle as evidence of these different authors (or faulty redaction), and the list of these apparent "mistakes" is quite long. Joel Rosenberg lists several examples under the category of "redundancy" when discussing biblical poetics. As Rosenberg reminds us:

> Adam names his wife twice. Noah is twice commanded to load the ark, once with "two of every kind," and once with seven pairs of every clean beast, and two each of every unclean. Abraham passes his wife off as a sister twice. Hagar is driven out of Abraham's household twice. Jacob "supplants" his brother Esau three times. Joseph is sold both to Midianites and Ishmaelites. The Israelites in the desert rebel against

Moses no less than seven times. Balaam tries three times to drive his donkey forward and three times to curse Israel. The Ten Commandments are given twice. Saul is elevated as king three times. And so on. (1984:42)

Proponents of source criticism argue that if the patriarch/wife/other narrative episodes in Genesis 12, 20, and 26 were the work of a single author, there would be serious rhetorical contradictions. E. A. Speiser, for example, argues that no competent writer would be guilty of the glaring faults evident in Abraham's characterization:

> Abraham learned nothing from his narrow escape in Egypt, and so tried the same ruse in Gerar [supposedly, after his first attempt misfires, Abraham would not be likely to make the same mistake again] . . . Abimelech, for his part, is so little sobered by his perilous experience with the first couple as to fall into the identical trap with the next pair . . . and Abimelech is depicted as both upright and wise. (1964:xxxi-xxxii)

As a result, source critics assume that the triplet resulted from varying treatments of a single original incident by different authors. Speiser, for example, assigns Gen 12:10-20 and Gen 26:1-22 to "J," and Genesis 20 to "E." Klaus Koch, on the other hand, considers "J" and "E" to be redactors of Gen 12:10-20 and Genesis 20, respectively, and "J" or "a second J source" to have redacted Gen 26:1-22 (1969:129-130). Hermann Gunkel has still another scenario: he assigns Gen 12:10-20 to "J," Gen 20:10-20 to "E," and the account in Genesis 26 to "J^R" (1966:1-5, 18-19, 40-41, 128-130). In addition, there is no unanimity as to which of the three is supposed to represent the "original" story. Koch believes that all three tales stem from an "Ur-version" and sets out to reconstruct a common original from the "oldest-seeming" elements in each extant version (1969:122). John Van Seters's view is that Genesis 20 is based on Genesis 12, and that Genesis 26 is based on chapters 12 and 20 (1975:177-183). Contrary to both Koch and Van Seters, E. Maly's position is that Genesis 26 provides the more "original" version (1956).

Several reasons are given for attributing these three narratives to different writers. Among them is the variation in the use of the divine names and differences in literary style. Speiser, for example, notes that Gen 12:10-20 is in the style of "traditional narrative," its generic elements simple and straightforward. The individual elements (Pharaoh/Egypt, plagues, hasty departure) lead Susan Niditch to conclude that it was composed after the formation of the Exodus tradition, its lack of bitterness toward foreign monarchs and particularly toward Egypt itself implying that this piece comes from a period of relative security, certainly from a period in which exodus and conquest are part of the past integrated into a literary topos (1987:62). Niditch also refers to the economical style of narration, consistent with the "J" writer. (Here Niditch's use of the term "economical" does not refer to the frequently encountered terseness of classical Hebrew prose—despite Gunkel's suggestion that such economical style "originated in the poverty of language" [1966:71], but to the fact that more often than not the same thought, image, or event is expressed in similar language throughout the narrative.) This "economy," or, to use Albert B. Lord's term, "thrift" (1968:53), emerges in the repeated language of Gen 12:11-13 (Abraham's request and explanation to Sarah), Gen 12:14-16 (the indication that events go exactly as planned), and Gen 12:19 (Pharaoh's interrogation of Abraham concerning the latter's "scheme"). Niditch also notes that "the traditionally J-style repetition whereby whole phrases recur at important narrative intervals" is absent in Genesis 20, in contrast to the style of Genesis 12, where repetition is a compositional tool.

However, many of these stylistic and linguistic "peculiarities" attributed to each source are being questioned. The complaint of the ruler *mah-zo't 'asîta lî/lanû* ("What is this you have done to me/us?") found in Gen 12:18 and 26:10, for example, is now generally accepted as idiomatic biblical Hebrew, routinely used to accuse a person of wrongdoing, and does not appear to belong specifically to a given source (see, e.g., Gen 29:25, Jacob questioning Laban; Exod 14:11, Israelites complaining to Moses; and Judg 15:11, men of Judah rebuking Samson). Similarly, Pharaoh's consternation with Abraham after the revelation of the hero's relationship to Sarah, conveyed by brief questions that wait for no answer ("What is this you have done to me? Why did you not tell me that she is your wife? Why did you say, 'She is my sister,' so that I took her for myself as a wife?" [12:18-19]) can as reasonably be attributed to narrative strategy (see discussion below) as evidence of J's "economical language."

The question of repetition is also being studied in light of contemporaneous ancient Near Eastern literary practices. As Umberto Cassuto discusses (1978), in the narrative tradition of the ancient Near East the occurrence of analogous tales is not uncommon.[2] Since the use of repetition was a customary feature of the narrative literature of the ancient East, it is not surprising that biblical narratives also show clear traces of this literary device. According to the literary concepts and norms of the ancient world, it appears that reiteration is desirable and characteristic.

ANTHROPOLOGICAL READINGS

Read as type-scenes, or what Michael Fishbane calls a "scenic-compound" (1985:11-12), these biblical "wife-as-sister" tales have been studied by scholars of other disciplines as well. Anthropologists have used these narratives for information about ancient Near Eastern tribal culture. Rosenberg, for example, claims that the "wife-as-sister" motif is important because it is one of several kinds of episodes which illustrate Abraham's contact with foreigners, and one in which the question of foreignness, as such, is most at issue. From this point on, "spouse = kin; foreigner = non-spouse" (1986:78). That is, Abraham's balanced endogamy contrasts with both the unbridled exogamy of the Egyptians/"Philistines" and the unbridled endogamy of Lot. Rosenberg explores the circumstantial exogamy of the Egyptians, as perceived by the narrator or his antecedent tradition, and notes that the Nile Delta and Canaanite communities, being the most urbanized and cosmopolitan environments of the region, would quite naturally be perceived as an erosive force to the tribal solidarity of more parochial visitors, and its marital practices as ipso facto "exogamous" (1986:233, n. 40). Niditch (1987) concurs, and views these narratives as an expression of deep concern about Israelite

31

identity, marriage inside and outside the group, the fear of incest, and the fear of foreigners. Niditch resolves the political conflicts in an interesting way. She notes that the Genesis 12 narrative is one of "fleeting contact and retreat, sustained distrust and marginality."

> In Gen 20:1-18, "us" meets "them" on equal footing, the heroes remaining and prospering in the alien world. . . . The wife-sister tales ultimately provide models for the ways in which the "us" and the "them," as variously defined, relate to one another in realms of social reality. (1987:66)

Other anthropological approaches have used the wife-as-sister theme to explain that the Hurrian society marriage bonds were strongest and most solemn when the wife had simultaneously the juridical status of a sister, regardless of actual blood ties. According to Speiser (1964:91), sometimes a man would marry a girl and at the same time adopt her as his sister. Violations of such sistership arrangements were punished more severely than breaches of marriage contracts, the practice apparently being a reflection of the underlying fratriarchal system which gave the adoptive brother greater authority than was granted the husband. By the same token, the adopted sister would enjoy correspondingly greater protection and higher social status.

Recent research in the Nuzi archives, as quoted by Nahum Sarna (1989:102-103), sheds some interesting perspectives. One document reads "Akkulenni son of Akiya . . . sold his sister Beltakkadummi as sister to Hurazzi of Ennaya," and another document records that according to a marriage-contract of "Akkulenni son of Akiya, contracted with Hurazzi son of Ennaya . . . Akkulenni shall give his sister Beltakkadummi as wife to Hurazzi." In other words, Beltakkadummi enjoyed the dual status of wife-sistership which endowed her with superior privileges and protection, over and above those of an ordinary wife. Accordingly, Sarna argues that Sarah and Rebekah were both holders of this wife-sister privilege, peculiar to the society from which they came and in which the legal aspects of their marriage were negotiated.

COMPARATIVE LITERATURE

Comparatists are interested also in these narratives, and note contemporaneous epics which provide parallels to the biblical motif of the abduction of the hero's beautiful wife. For example, there is a Canaanite narrative of King Kertet who lost his "lovely spouse Hurrai," through whom he was supposed to be destined to carry on his line. He had to mount a military campaign to recover her. In Greek literature, there is Helen of Troy, who was kidnapped twice, once in her youth by Theseus and again after she married Menelaus. In fact, it was her abduction to Troy by Paris which caused the Trojan War. Another strikingly similar incident is found in the Egyptian "Tale of Two Brothers," in which Bata's beautiful second wife "miraculously" comes to the attention of Pharaoh, who has her hunted down and brought to his palace. There he makes love to her, even though he knows she is married. Comparatists note that it is reasonable to assume that similar sagas circulated about the matriarchs of Israel, and were collected and incorporated into the patriarchal narratives. Presumably, the uncommon beauty of the progenitrix of Israel was a matter of national pride, as were the comings and goings of the patriarchs at the courts of kings.

THEOLOGICAL INTEREST

Finally, of course, these wife-as-sister narratives have been viewed from a theological perspective. Several theologians argue that Genesis 20 and 26 are moral revisions of the core tradition in Genesis 12, the earlier narrative reflecting the sensuality and immorality of the pagan nations, while the latter two emphasize God's direct, protective intervention. Robert Polzin, for example, finds recurring messages in the three versions concerning adultery, wealth, progeny, and *God's blessing* (1975). Samuel Sandmel (1961:110-111) and Koch (1969:123-125), bothered by the lacunae in Genesis 12 regarding Abraham's motivations, the purity of Sarah, *the role of God*, and the responsibility of the foreign king, claim that the authors of Gen 20:1-18 and Gen 26:1-17 reinterpreted the original narrative and transformed it in the light of their particular interests. Similarly, Baruch Halpern claims that the variations in the three narratives represent deliberate distortions of puzzling or unacceptable texts. According to Halpern, Genesis 20 is a variant of picaresque episodes in Genesis 12 and 26. In Genesis 20, God is acquitted of treating Abraham's innocent dupe unfairly (20:4-6; cf. 12:17). But, more important, Abraham is defended (by appeal to literal, or what we might call technical, grounds [20:12]) against the charge that he lied. Since the moral justification offered in all three versions (12:11-13; 20:11; 26:7) is regarded as insufficient to bear the weight of Abraham's lie, the author of Genesis 20 has *consciously* reworked his materials to expunge the potential blot from Abraham's character (1983:62). (Read this way, a hagiographic bent determines the manner in which the author supplements his source!)

Clearly, scholars of many disciplines eagerly acknowledge the relationship of Genesis 12, 20, and 26.

BIBLICAL INTERTEXTUALITY

Since the techniques of post-structuralist literary critics have been appropriated by our discipline, sequential narrative episodes which reflect upon each other are described now as "intertextual" and are being studied from a literary perspective.[3] Intertextuality allows that prior readings are not errors to be discarded (contra source critics), but instead reveal repetitions of textual structures.

Biblical intertextuality exists on both micro- and macro-levels. On the smallest linguistic level (individual words and phrases), the relationship is easily recognizable. Repetitions and shifts represent the basis for a wealth of scholarly material. The study of lexical similarities and differences is, in fact, one of the mainstays of biblical criticism. Adele Berlin, among others, explores how "lexical cohesion" (the ways in which words are linguistically connected within a sequence) plays a role in interpretation, and how awareness of this relationship can lead to better readings (1989). In a very different kind of criticism, Harold Bloom (1976) examines "poetic crossings," the ways in which a text can destroy its own integrity if examined within the framework of lexical similarities and differences.

Biblical scholars have studied intertextuality on a larger level as well. "Type-scenes" are intertextual in that they relate narrative events using fixed modes or sequences of action. However, type-scenes are most often discussed in the context of the biblical *writer's* ability to shape the text, rather than the *reader's* role in interpreting it. James G. Williams (1980), for example, suggests that Genesis 12, 20, and 26 exemplify variations on the formulaic convention "the wife/sister scene," and explores the way in which each *author* uniquely employs the basic pattern, emphasizing that elusive "authorial intention." Similarly, Robert C. Culley (1976) outlines the patterns of content found in each account of the wife-sister tale, contrasts and compares them, and provides a review of scholarship on oral narrative, again focusing on the *author*ship of folkloric material.

Biblical "typology" is also intertextual, since characters and scenes symbolically pre-figure later events (most often, the "Old Testament" is read as a prefiguration of the events of the "New"). Of course, the Hebrew Bible also has several self-contained examples of typology. Rosenberg points out the following:

> The parting of the waters of Creation anticipates the parting of the Reed (or "Red") Sea for Israel. The escape of Noah in an ark (*tevah*) anticipates the escape of the infant Moses in a cradle (*tevah*) on the Nile. The descent of Abraham to Egypt in time of famine and his exit from Egypt with great wealth anticipate the events of the Exodus story. The building of the desert tabernacle anticipates the building of the Temple in the days of Solomon. . . . (1984:51)

Thus, intertextuality exists on several levels, not only in narratives which seem repetitive.

INTERTEXTUALITY AND TRANSFERENCE: HOW DO THEY RELATE?

Recently, another interest of post-structuralist literary critics has been explored by our discipline: the *process* by which individual readers confer meaning and perceive intertextuality. One explanation is transference, a concept long recognized in the psychoanalytic process, and an activity quite similar to that of reading. The relationship of a reader and a text replicates that of analyst and analysand, interpreter and code. The roles of analyst and analysand in reading, however, are not as clearly defined as in the psychoanalytic process because the status of that which is analyzed, the text, is not that of a patient. That is to say, the text has authority, the very type of authority by which Jacques Lacan (1977) defines the role of the *analyst* in the structure of transference. Just as the analysand views the analyst as "a subject presumed to know," so a reader approaches a text as "the very place where meaning, and *knowledge* of meaning, reside" (Felman 1980a:7). Thus, a reader simultaneously occupies the place of analyst *and* the place of analysand.

According to the psychoanalytic account of transference, the structures of the unconscious are revealed by the analyst's encounters with the analysand's discourse. The analyst, in effect, repeats the experience described by the analysand and thereby gains particular insight into the analysand's psychical life. Thus transference is a repetition linking the analyst to the analysand. Similarly, reading is a repetition of the text it seeks to analyze. Prior readings, particularly those which have narrative similarity, are not errors to be discarded, but revealing recurrences of textual structures. It is through transference, then, that the analysand tries to force or coax the analyst to play out a scene he or she has in mind. As a result, this self-reflexiveness does not produce or induce a closure in which the text is the thing it describes, but rather leads to a multiplicity of representations, a plurality of meanings. And plurality, here, does not mean *several* meanings, but rather that the text cannot be reduced to *a* meaning.

Intertextuality allows that all texts are reflections of all other texts. That is, they all contribute to the production of meaning because they have already been read (or as Julia Kristeva writes, "Every text is the absorption and transformation of other texts" [1971:146]). A reader *of* the text exists since a work can be read only in connection with or against other texts. The method by which this occurs is transference: a reader is caught up in and reenacts the drama he or she thought was being analyzed from the outside (a reader *in* the text). Intertextuality and transference work, in effect, to divide the text against itself, creating a need for response and a response to the need. Meaning is simultaneously within the text and outside it, hence a reader *in/of* the text.

The relationship between intertextuality and transference, a "reader-*of*-the-text" and a "reader-*in*-the-text," lies in the dynamic interaction between text and reader, free-ranging play of mind on one hand and organizing response on the other. Like analysis, reading is a two-part process consisting of disorganization and reorganization, taking the text apart and putting it back together again. Janus-faced, a reader looks back in the text for clues to explain ambiguities while simultaneously looking toward future possibilities and larger patterns, based on individual response (thus involving both intertextuality and transference). Textual duplications lead to larger motifs, and tentative explorations in different directions condense into one focused moment, not to provide the *authoritative* interpretation, but rather to afford new perspectives, find new relationships, change emphases. A reader re-creates a text, combining intertextual episodes with his or her own characteristic processes of mind (transference). By focusing on evasions, ambivalences, and points of intensity in the narrative—words which do not get spoken, words which are spoken with unusual frequency, doublings, etc.—a reader in/of the text finds a "sub-text" which the work both conceals and reveals. A reader focuses simultaneously on the text itself (common rhetorical or stylistic features, its intertextuality) and the response to the text (transference).

Reading, as analysis, thus relies on two simple strategies: on the one hand, paying attention to everything, and, on the other, mistrusting seemingly obvious implications; that is, being open to the sudden switches and rearrangements that reveal alternate messages and expose the dynamic play of meaning behind what may seem to be a simple statement. For a reader in/of the text, interpretation does not proceed from partial to definitive meaning and then come to rest, but instead is an ongoing process. Elements of narrative cohesion constantly shift, blurring the distinctions between provisional and "fulfilled" meanings, between shadows and truth. Reading, like analysis, becomes an activity of repressing and reconstructing, of forgetting and remembering, and that activity, by its very nature, resists completion. A reader confers meaning retrospectively; earlier narrative elements retain a provisional status until a reader reaches another meaning based upon subsequent episodes. Intertextuality and transference become interdependent, for the very notion of fulfillment suggests that things must be fulfilled and are not yet.[4]

It may sound as if I am invoking Freud to justify the kind of free associational play in biblical scholarship that recently has become familiar in literary studies. Indeed, when Freud came to America in 1908, with his strange discoveries about the way the mind works, he warned, "I bring you the plague." Certainly, current literary criticism has plagues of its own, whether caught from Freud or not. And, of course, there is a certain irony in the application of literary theory to biblical texts. Lynn Poland (1990), among others, discusses some of the difficulties involved in applying literary criticism to biblical texts (and the tensions which have developed in the academy as a result), particularly with regard to a unified "intention" on the part of the biblical writers. On the one hand, literary critics view texts as disunified, deconstructed, or in the Lacanian model, a hodgepodge of disconnected symbols. Yet, at the same time, they paradoxically welcome the acceptance of the biblical text as a "quasi-unified whole" in order to "rescue" the Bible from source critics.[5] The problem seems to be polar thinking: either texts make meaning and readers are superfluous, or readers make meaning and texts are superfluous. But neither makes meaning alone. It is not texts *or* readers; it is texts *and* readers, the relationship of intertextuality (reader-*of*-the-text) and transference (reader-*in*-the-text). A reader is no more autonomous than a text; rather, reader and text are interdependent. Hence reader in/of the biblical text.

Since this self-reflexivity also occurs in subsequent readings of the same narrative, obvious intertextual episodes trigger transference to larger motifs, and as a result, individual narratives are read within the context of the larger biblical story, rather than as discrete tales or moral historiographies. One particular biblical narrative episode can be read only in connection *with* or *against* another. The plot develops and events become sequential rather than redundant, providing a grid through which antecedent scenes are re-examined, not to enhance an initial impression, but rather to qualify and complicate it.

Thus, it is impossible to segregate sections of the Bible away from the exegetical practice of reading it intertextually. As Berlin points out:

> Understanding a passage in the Bible, like understanding any discourse, is largely a matter of understanding the relationship between its parts. When the parts hang together, the discourse is coherent and can be interpreted. When a relationship between the parts cannot be discerned, the discourse lacks coherence; it does not make sense, and so cannot be interpreted. (1989:29)

As a result, for readers of the Hebrew Bible, there is never a beginning, only a *berē'shît* ("when, in the beginning" [Gen 1:1]).

Reading within this larger text, the patriarch/wife/other motif goes beyond obviously related tales to resound a larger pattern: patriarch/wife/other becomes powerful male/powerless female/uninvited sex. A male is willing to sacrifice a female who is *ostensibly* important to him; the sacrifice of the powerless female usually involves sex; and the male becomes more powerful as a result of this forced prostitution.[6] In these Genesis narratives, oxymoronically one can hear echoes of female voicelessness and its attendant sexual danger or violence, echoes of Lot's two daughters, offered by their father to be raped by all the men of the city in order to spare the divine messengers (who are clearly capable of defending themselves) from this threatened fate (see chapter 4, below); also Hagar, Abraham's powerless concubine,[7] and of course the unnamed concubine of Judges, who was raped, mutilated, and left for dead.[8]

DISCOURSE ANALYSIS

As in psychoanalysis, the relationship of intertextuality and transference in Genesis 12 and 20 becomes most apparent when examining the discourse in these episodes. In the process, textual speech-acts and the narrator's comments extend the narrow wife-sister tale to the broader motif of powerful male/powerless female/uninvited sex.

It is difficult to distinguish the strictly rhetorical elements of discourse from other dimensions of the text, since hidden wishes or conflicts are always part of the latent content.[9] Of course, while a reader cannot overlook the importance of sheer communication embedded within a text—that between characters or a character's internal thoughts—as in the psychoanalytic use of *transference*, it is equally dangerous to ignore the exchange between speaker and listener, between text and reader. Similarly, *intertextuality* allows a reader, like a psychoanalyst, to draw certain conclusions based on frequency of specific word choice. Thus, although discourse analysis belongs to many fields, it seems particularly appropriate to psychoanalytic literary study, for words can mean more than they seem to mean and do more than they seem to do. The significance of words may even lie in the simple fact that they are utterances, regardless of content or presentation. As Freud notes:

> Words were originally magic and to this day words have retained much of their ancient magical power. By words one person can make another blissfully happy or drive him to despair, by words . . . the speaker determines . . . judgements and decisions. Words provoke affects and are in general the means of mutual influence. . . . (1916-17:17)

Examining discourse extends the discussion in linguistic circles about the relationship between gender, language, and social structure. There is a curiosity about and compelling concern with the question of who speaks in given situations: discourse is often understood as a form of domination, with speech use as an index of social values and the distribution of power. In Genesis 12 and 20 it is through his discourse that Abraham turns his less propitious circumstances to a higher level of success and social elevation. Abraham's marginality and insecurity are replaced by wealth and a more stable status—at the cost of sacrificing Sarah. Through *transference*, a repetition which links analyst and patient, reader and text, a reader, like an analyst, repeats the experience described and thereby gains particular insight.

The converse of speech—silence—is equally meaningful, since the character who is denied discourse often experiences narrative suppression as well. As Ruth Bottigheimer (1987:52) discusses, speech and silencing exist on four levels in a literary text: narrative, textual, lexical, and editorial. The character who is condemned or cursed to a period of silence experiences narrative silencing in the plot. The distribution of direct and indirect or reported speech offers the potential for silencing a character at a second, textual level. Silencing may also grow out of verbs used to introduce direct or indirect speech (certain verbs validate the speech that follows, while other introductory verbs mark subsequent speech as illicit). Finally, the author or editor may comment on the text within the text. Sarah, the wife, is silenced on all four of these levels, and *transference* "triggers" a response—frustration—in me as a reader.

POWERFUL MALE/POWERLESS FEMALE

Both Genesis 12 and 20 are told from the male point of view. Except for the indirect quotation of Gen 20:5, Sarah neither speaks nor takes any action. Even the discourse of the other characters negates her individuality: not one of them refers to Sarah by name, only by personal pronoun or as the property of Abraham. Pharaoh's identification of Sarah is "she," "your wife," "her." Abimelech identifies Sarah as "she," "she herself," or "your wife." Abraham tells Abimelech "she is my sister" rather than identifying Sarah by name. Even God has this anonymous view: Abimelech dreams that God tells him he is a dead man for having taken a *be'ulat-ba'al*. Although this expression is translated usually as "a man's wife," its literal meaning is the "possession of a possessor," the more usual word for "wife" being *'ishah*. Since the expression *be'ulat-ba'al* is used rarely, and primarily in negative situations,[10] textual repetition—*intertextuality*—combines with the process of *trans-ference* to force a reader to recognize Sarah as powerless. As a result, analyst and analysand (interpreter and code, reader and text) are linked, and change roles: a reader *of* the text becomes a reader *in* the text. That is, specific word choice highlights the fact that *intertextuality* and *transference*, working together, allow, indeed *require*, a reader to be caught up in and reenact the drama. Sarah is silenced and so am I; indeed, so is any reader who identifies with her.

Abraham, on the other hand, has speech, and his first discourse contains both his proposal to Sarah and his rationale:

> I know that you are a beautiful woman, and when the Egyptians see you, they will say, "This is his wife." They will slay me, but they will let you live. Please say you are my sister, that it may go well with me because of you, and that my life may be spared on your account. (Gen 12:11-13)

Abraham's initial argument here is narrow and truncated. He claims to fear that the Egyptians will kill him because Sarah is beautiful. It seems strange, however, that Abraham would entertain these fears since, according to what we are told later, Sarah is only ten years younger than Abraham, that is, sixty-five years old.[11] Nor is it evident what Abraham hopes to gain by presenting Sarah as his sister. C. F. Keil and F. Delitzsch (1971) claim that Abraham will be in a better position to protect Sarah as her brother than as her husband, but Abraham says nothing about her protection. John Skinner (1930) argues that the Egyptians would be likely to see a beautiful woman and murder her husband so that one of them can have her, but this assumes that in ancient Egypt murder is preferable to committing adultery.

In any event, Abraham's discourse does not include a discussion about any presumed Egyptian immorality. Abraham's expressed concern is for himself, despite the "logical" argument he presents. While his rationale is that the Egyptians will kill him and let Sarah live, he says nothing about the predicament Sarah could be in by masquerading as his sister (see Miscall 1983:32). Abraham's discourse seems to explain that residence in a foreign place with his wife will result in his murder. For

Abraham, beauty, desire, and murder are connected. The first two necessarily and inevitably lead to the third. But the murder Abraham explicitly states that he fears is averted by his deception, at the cost of Sarah being taken as Pharaoh's wife. And there seems to be little doubt that sexual intercourse occurred since Pharaoh states directly, "I took her to me as a wife" (Gen 12:19). The same phrase was used in reference to Abraham taking Hagar, and that action resulted in the birth of Ishmael.

Since discourse often reflects hidden desires, perhaps Abraham's real motive is to receive gifts from the Egyptians, and his words "that it may go well with me because of you" are a euphemistic way of saying that by abandoning his wife to the lust of a foreign potentate, he might derive material advantage. Certainly Abraham shows no regard for Sarah's welfare, as his language demonstrates ("so that it may go well with me . . . that *my* soul may live . . ."). Perhaps Abraham sees Sarah as expendable because she has no child, and thus wants to be rid of her as a wife. Or, perhaps Abraham is not concerned about Sarah because he views Lot as his descendant. According to Clines (1990:70), since Lot appears to be the only possible candidate for the fulfillment of the promise of progeny to Abraham, Sarah is disposable: "Nothing hangs upon her continued survival."

Significantly Abraham uses the verb *harog*, best translated as "slay" and connoting ruthless brutality.[12] This serves to draw attention to his exaggerated fears and to convince Sarah—and through transference a reader—to participate in his subterfuge. Abraham devises the plan so that all will be to his advantage, ignoring Sarah's potential danger.

Although many commentators argue that Sarah is an accomplice in Abraham's plan,[13] discourse analysis allows that Sarah's role is due more to her powerlessness than to her willing agreement. Sarah does not speak in this episode, and the narrator offers no comments on her feelings, her response, or what she says to Pharaoh. Her silence is not an indication of complicity, but of helplessness. Sarah is not a co-conspirator, but rather a silent object, a pawn, and is effectively suppressed. Just as the analyst, through *transference*, may actually experience the emotions of the patient, so too will a reader, who feels Sarah's anguish and helplessness.

THE "OTHER"

When Pharaoh discovers the deception, he cites what *Abraham*, and Abraham alone, has said to him (12:19). Abraham, the protagonist, chosen by God, is contrasted with Pharaoh who, from the beginning of the scene, is depicted as just. It is Pharaoh, not Abraham, who is concerned about the consequences of adultery. It is Pharaoh, not Abraham, who discerns that the plagues were sent because of Sarah's exploitation. Even when Pharaoh remonstrates against Abraham, he does not mention the hardship of the plagues but rather stresses the wrong of Abraham's action. By placing the condemnation against Abraham in the mouth of Pharaoh, the contrast between the foreigner who seems well acquainted with the demands of this deity and Abraham who does not is overwhelming. And once again, *transference* allows me as a reader to identify with a narrative character—this time with Pharaoh.

The antagonist's scolding of the protagonist, "Why did you not tell me that she is your wife?" (Gen 12:18), expresses a clear attitude of opposition to sexual exploitation, an assumption that all people are subject to this ethical precept, even kings. *Intertextuality*, however, raises the possibility that perhaps only foreign kings are held to this level of morality, if the women-stealing tendencies of kings in 1 Samuel 8 are any indication. Certainly, in Genesis 12, a foreign monarch is shown to be more fastidious than the Judean patriarch!

The foreign ruler's speech to Abraham is impassioned, and transference *forces* me as a reader to react similarly. Pharaoh speaks quickly, in a series of accusatory statements that leave Abraham no time to respond. Indeed, Abraham, whose artful discourse convinces Sarah to pose as his sister, can only remain silent as he faces his accuser, Pharaoh, who is completely correct in his accusations:

> What is this you have done to me? Why did you not tell me
> that she is your wife? Why did you say, "She is my sister," so

that I took her to me as a wife? And now, Look at your wife!
Take and go! (Gen 12:18-19)

In these two verses Pharaoh stresses Sarah's relationship to
Abraham, a relationship Abraham is content to abrogate. Sarah
is Abraham's wife, and Pharaoh, like this reader, is shocked that
Abraham would sexually exploit her. Pharaoh's repulsion over
Abraham's actions is revealed in the very words of his demand
that Abraham leave: "take" (*laqaḥ*) normally requires an object
or a prepositional phrase; by omitting it Pharaoh's speech is
even more impassioned.[14]

AND YET AGAIN!
OR, INTERTEXTUALITY AND TRANSFERENCE

Intertextuality and *transference* now allow me as a reader in/of
this text to confer meaning to the second part of Gen 12:16
("And he had sheep, oxen . . ."): it is a retroactive explanation,
in detail, of the first part of that same verse, "and Abraham was
well treated." That is, these gifts are the foundation of Abraham's wealth. Again, just as *transference* is a repetition which
links the analyst to the analysand, so reading is a repetition of
the text it seeks to analyze. Prior readings, like prior actions, are
not errors to be discarded, but important revelations. In this
case, the revelation is that Abraham benefits materially by
prostituting his wife,[15] and because his ruse is so successful, he
has Sarah pose as his sister once again, this time in Gerar
(Genesis 20).

Now his actions are even more appalling, primarily because
of the narrative context. In Genesis 12, there is little or no
chance that Sarah would become pregnant even if Pharaoh did
have sexual relations with her. By chapter 20, however, readers
know that Sarah will have a child in less than a year.[16] God
had promised Abraham, and Sarah learns of the promise when
she overhears Abraham's recollection of the conversation (see
chapter 5, below). In fact, the very next scene tells of Sarah's
pregnancy and the birth of Isaac. Abraham is fully culpable in
placing Sarah in the position of being violated by another man.
Indeed, if she *had* stayed with Abimelech, even the paternity of

her child would have been in doubt, and any adulterous relationship would have had serious consequences: Sarah found in
the harem of Abimelech to be pregnant with another man's
child would mean certain death.

Unless Abraham's material gain is considered a motive,
Abraham's exploitation of Sarah a second time is unfathomable.
Unlike the earlier episode, when famine compels the couple to
travel, there is no explanation for their sojourn in Gerar. Further, Abraham does not claim to fear being killed because of
Sarah's beauty as he did when he approached Egypt, which
casts doubts upon his later rationale to Abimelech.

Since, according to transference, the structures of the
unconscious are revealed by discourse, Abimelech's words are
as significant as Pharaoh's in revealing motivations and stimu-
lating a reader's response. Like Pharaoh, he chooses his words
well when speaking to both God and Abraham. He appeals to
God's sense of justice and professes his innocence. He proves
to the deity, and due to *transference* to me as a reader, that
Abraham lied to him. *Intertextuality* enforces this perception of
Abimelech—the king employs the solemn oath used throughout
the Hebrew Bible "in the integrity of my heart," to reiterate his
innocence (see, e.g., 1 Kgs 9:4 and Pss 78:72; 101:2). In a
series of pointed questions, he berates Abraham four times,
without even pausing to hear his reply. Only in the last question
does he leave time for Abraham to answer, demanding, "What
did you see that you did this thing?" (Gen 20:10). Because of
transference, I must ask the same question.

Abraham responds with weak excuses. What is striking in a
narrative filled with moral discourse between Abimelech and
God is the absence of a similar position in Abraham. While
Abimelech accuses Abraham of bringing a great sin upon him
and upon his kingdom, and of "doing things which should not
be done," Abraham does not respond to Abimelech's actual
questions, and neither the narrator nor God makes any comment on Abraham's reprehensible actions. Indeed, God's
actions in these narratives are certainly difficult to reconcile. He
punishes Pharaoh, Abimelech, and their houses, but not Abraham. In fact, immediately after the encounter with Abimelech,

the Lord "visits" Sarah, and she bears Isaac (Gen 21:1-5). Perhaps the text is questioning the very notion of causality.[17]

Throughout this episode, Abraham gives inaccurate information and his words are suspect. First, Abraham claims he perpetrated the deception because there was "no fear of God in this place" (Gen 20:11). Yet there seemed to be *substantial* "fear of God" on the part of both Abimelech and his servants.

Second, Abraham's discourse contradicts *even this* excuse. Abraham claims that he had asked Sarah "at *every* place [and not just those places that lack a 'fear of God'] . . . say of me, 'He is my brother.'"

Third, Abraham claims that Sarah is actually his half-sister.[18] Although Speiser holds that this provides Sarah's "legitimate" genealogical information, "the ultimate purpose [of which is] to establish the superior strain of the line" (1964:93), and Adin Steinsaltz reads "my sister" as a reference to the "chief-wife" as opposed to other, secondary wives (1984:22), Abraham's assertion that Sarah is his blood relative is confirmed neither by the narrator nor by any other dialogue or genealogical source either before or after this scene. Despite the fact that Sarah *may* come from the same ancestral land as Abraham, and despite the fact that Abraham *may* be using the term "sister" as one of endearment, such usage apparently common in early Eastern cultures (Songs 5:1, 2), Abraham's story that she is his *half*-sister is, at the very least, suspect.

Finally, Abraham states that God "caused me to wander" (Gen 20:13). Significantly, however, if read from a Freudian perspective, Abraham's word choice was *not* deceptive. The verb he uses, *hit'û*, not only means "cause to wander" but also "mislead" (see, e.g., Isa 3:12; 9:15; Hos 4:11). And there is no doubt that Abraham has "misled" Pharaoh, Abimelech, Sarah, and me. As a result, there is certainly irony in Abraham's remark that he asked Sarah to describe him as her brother because of her *ḥesed*, a word usually translated as "loyalty."[19]

Intertextuality and *transference*, combined, highlight Abraham's lack of concern for Sarah, his willingness to sacrifice his wife for his own material gain. *Intertextuality*, reenforcing the concept that narrative recurrences are not errors, emphasizes that as a wife represented as a sister, Sarah obtains riches and safety for Abraham: Abimelech, like Pharaoh increases Abraham's wealth and social standing. At the same time, as a sister discovered to be a wife, Sarah creates an indebtedness on the part of the abductors to the husband who lent his wife in the first place. Both ways, the husband gains and the abductor is off the hook. *Transference* forces me as a reader to experience emotions. In this case, Sarah remains degraded as an object and I must share her anguish. Her beauty and status initially attract and protect, then become the cause of calamity. The irony is that Pharaoh, Abimelech, and I as a reader understand the immorality of adultery, and the crime of female sexual sacrifice, more readily than Abraham.

Sandmel (1961) suggests that the tales exemplify inner-biblical aggadah, that is, one version "corrects" and explains another. And for me as a reader in/of the text, the tales *do* exemplify inner-biblical aggadah; the tales *do* explain one another. The reason for Abraham's deception is buried rhetorically deep within the resolution of the larger biblical narrative, a part of the dénouement rather than the opening motivation. When Abraham offers the excuse that Sarah is indeed his half-sister, and that throughout their travels they have made public only one side of their family relationship as a precaution, he perceives his actions as nothing more than a minor deception.

Here *intertextuality* and *transference* affect something far more fundamental than the characters' experiences or the plot alone: they affect this reader as well. By reading in/of the text, I have become wary of that infamous "referential fallacy" (Riffaterre 1978) with a heightened sensitivity to all the ways in which conventional, literal-minded expectations about meaning are defeated. The most scandalous thing about Abraham's ignominious actions is that, as readers, we are forced to participate; a reader's innocence cannot remain intact, since there can be no such thing as an innocent reader of this text. The scandal is not simply in the text, but resides in a reader's relation to the text. What is most outrageous is not simply that of which the text is speaking, but that which makes it speak to this reader.

3

WHOSE DREAM IS THIS, ANYWAY? ABIMELECH'S INTERPRETATION OF A DREAM AND A DREAM OF INTERPRETATION

We experience every sort of thing in dreams and believe in it.
—Sigmund Freud (1916-17:90)

In this chapter I focus on two things. First, I explore psychoanalytic dream theory as a model for reading Abimelech's dream in Genesis 20. Psychoanalysts treat "daydreams" and "night dreams" quite differently, asking different questions about them and using different language to describe them. Generally speaking, in discussing "daydreams" analysts look for conflicts among the dreamer's id, ego, and superego. In "night dreams"[1] (like the one in Genesis 20), however, analysts look for conflicts between conscious and unconscious ideas. Because Abimelech's dream in Genesis is a "night dream," this is the model which I explore in this chapter.[2]

The Freudian theory of "night dreams," commonly referred to as his "topographical model," is a particularly useful tool in literary criticism since night dreams defy not only "reality," but also the ordinary means of *representing* reality. That is, dreams often contain peculiar images and bizarre language which need to be interpreted. The way we interpret dreams can be an effective tool for understanding the way certain literary texts work, particularly narratives *about* dreams. And tales of dreamers abound in ancient Near Eastern literature. Indeed, the importance and frequency of kings' dreams are well recognized,[3] and the "bad dream/consultation-with-courtiers" motif in Genesis 20 is found also in other biblical foreign court tales, such as those about Joseph and Daniel.[4]

The second focus of this chapter, like the rest of this book, is *about* reading. What does Genesis 20 have to say about its own creation? What in the text invites interpretation, and what in the text resists it? How, through reading, does the narrative act itself out? And how do I, as a reader, get caught in Abimelech's dream and participate with him in its interpretation? In other words, how do the text and I collaborate in its creation?

Although it is Abraham's discourse with the Philistines which sets the plot in motion and his intercession with God to heal Abimelech and his household which ends the episode, it is Abimelech tracing his dream back to past desires which enables me as a reader to weigh its significance to future biblical narrative events. As Shoshana Felman notes (in a very different context), whichever way a reader turns, he or she cannot avoid being turned by the text; he or she must *perform* it by *repeating* it (1980b:101). That is, although it is Abimelech's dream, by *reading* the narrative we repeat Abimelech's interpretive process.

ABIMELECH'S DREAM

Genesis 20 begins with the information that Abraham, having arrived in Gerar, has once again resorted to the subterfuge of claiming that his wife, Sarah, is his sister (see chapter 2, above). As a result, Abimelech, the king of Gerar, incorporates Sarah into his household. One night Abimelech has a dream which consists of a conversation between God and himself. In the morning, the king consults his courtiers and then upbraids Abraham for having deceived him. The chapter ends with Abraham praying to the deity (as foretold in Abimelech's dream) and the narrator's report that God "healed" Abimelech, his wife, and his female slaves so that they all bore children, sexual dysfunction having been an apparent restraint.

There seems to be little controversy over the parameters of the narrative events which surround Abimelech's dream, but the exact verses which constitute the dream itself are not clear. Most commentators read the dream narrative as all of Gen 20:3-7. Read this way, one night Abimelech dreamed that he and the deity had a conversation. In this dream, God said to him, "Look! You are a dead man because of the woman you took. She is a man's wife." The narrative account of the dream is interrupted by the narrator who interjects that Abimelech had not come near Sarah. Abimelech's dream then continues with his response: "Lord, will you slay even a righteous nation? Did he not say to me 'She is my sister'? She, *even she* said, 'He is my brother.' In the innocence of my heart and in the purity of my hands I did this." God responds: "*I* know that in the innocence of your heart you did this. It was *I* who withheld you from sinning against me. That is why I did not let you touch her. Now, restore the man's wife. Because he is a prophet he will pray for you, and you will live. But if you fail to restore her, know that you will surely die, you and all that is yours." At this point Abimelech awakens.

I would like to propose another reading, one based on Freud's psychoanalytic model. From this perspective, only verse 3 is the *actual* dream (God says to Abimelech: "Look! You are a dead man because of the woman you took. She is a man's wife")[5] and is an example of the very primitive, fantasy-based primary-process of dream-work called "condensation" and "displacement" (discussed below). End of dream. As Hillel might have said about verses 4-7, "the rest is commentary."

Rather than being part of the actual dream, Gen 20:4-7 reflects two later stages of dream work. Verses 4-5 represent that confusing stage of dream-work called "secondary-process" (which I examine in greater detail later). During this stage, generic opposites such as fantasy/reality, abstinence/lust, punishment/reward mingle, and these two verses clearly reflect this confusion:

> Abimelech had not come near her. He said, "Lord! Even a righteous nation will you slay? Did he not say to me 'She is my sister'? She, even she said, 'He is my brother.' In the

integrity of my heart and the innocence of my hands I did this."

Verses 6-7 represent the later process of dream-work, waking (also discussed below), the stage during which Abimelech *himself* translates his dream images of verse 3 into a coherent narrative, in effect interpreting his own dream, and resolving the confusion of verses 4-5:

> I [God] know that you did this in the integrity of your heart. I also withheld you from sinning against me. Therefore I did not permit you to touch her. Now, return the man's wife because he is a prophet and he will pray for you and you will live. If you do not return her know that you will surely die. You, and all that is yours.

How does dream theory work in this context? The basic outline of Abimelech's dream is simple: God speaks to the king, charging him with the abduction of a married woman and threatening him with death. Rhetorically and linguistically, God's words make a very forceful statement. But why would Abimelech have this dream? After all, the king knows that he has not violated Sarah. Indeed, God's opening words in the dream would highlight Abimelech's confusion: *hinneka*, often translated as "Behold!" emphatically marks this statement as an *unexpected* turn of events.[6] In effect, God is saying, "Guess what? Surprise! You are a dead man because of the woman you took . . ."

CENSORSHIP

In *The Interpretation of Dreams* (1900a), Freud explains that dreams fulfill repressed desires by allowing the unconscious to communicate to the conscious. The unconscious sends overwhelming urges upon the sleeper's mind, "condensing" a set of images into a single picture, and "displacing" the meaning of one object onto another. Freud describes these dream images as "primitive hieroglyphics" (1900a:132), the signs of which are to be individually "translated" into a creative story, or what is remembered as a "dream," by the preconscious or conscious mind. These raw materials are context-bound and cannot be analyzed in isolation. As Freud observes, "The same piece of content may conceal a different meaning when it occurs in various people or in various contexts" (1900a:137), and must be "inserted into the psychical chain that has to be traced backwards" (Freud 1900a:133). That is, the meaning of a dream, like that of a literary text, varies according to the language and culture of the dreamer or reader, and can be understood only retrospectively. The dreamer must decipher symbols which have no fixed meaning just as a reader must interpret signifiers, words, which are essentially indeterminate.

This primary-process of dream-work, with its characteristic turns analogous to figures of speech, simultaneously presents and distorts, represents and misrepresents, opposing actual dream images and concealed meanings.

In Freudian theory, dreams result from an unconscious impulse seeking fulfillment, a desire not actually fulfilled in waking life.[7] But the *figurative* activity of a dream (what analysts call the "latent" content, or the "forbidden" dream-thoughts) does not stand for its *literal* contents (referred to as "manifest contents," or the dream stories which the dreamer remembers). Instead, the dream is a *symbolic* fulfillment of unconscious wishes, a transformation of the dreamer's forbidden desires. In other words, an unconscious wish meets up with a preconscious thought and strives for an illusory satisfaction. But *why* are these unconscious wishes distorted in dream-images?

According to Freud, it is due to "censorship," the force of repression which exists at the edge between the unconscious and the preconscious and which will not allow these powerfully charged thoughts to surface in their original form. Part of a dreamer's reaction to censorship derives from sleep's paralyzing effect on the motor end of psychic apparatus, and a "forbidden" idea is stripped somewhat of its dangerous capacity to influence action. As Donald Moss writes,

> Detached from an active, erotic, body, the dreamer is also detached from that active body's linguistic proxy, syntax. Syntax mediates the formal demands of time, place and person. Such demands turn superfluous as the erotic body,

paralyzed with sleep, turns superfluous. Sentence, unobliged
to that body's spatial/temporal coordinates, unravels into
rebus. (1989:357)

In other words, under the influence of censorship, the "subversive" material of the latent dream thought is transformed into a
series of images, and that series of images is the manifest
dream. Hence Freud's dictum: "A dream is a (disguised) fulfillment of a (suppressed or repressed) wish" (1900a:160).[8]

What are Abimelech's unconscious wishes? How does
Abimelech's dream-work work? It would appear that in Genesis
20 the king's unconscious desire is sexual possession of Sarah,
the woman he "took." Read this way, verse 3 of the chapter
represents Abimelech's repressed and "forbidden" dream
thoughts, as modified—nearly beyond recognition—by "condensation" and "displacement."

CONDENSATION AND DISPLACEMENT

According to Freud, the first part of dream-work is *condensation*. That is, the manifest dream (the story which the dreamer
remembers) has a smaller content than the latent one (the
"forbidden" dream-thoughts). Although the manifest dream is
an "abbreviated translation" of the latent dream-thoughts,
condensation is far from being a simple process of merely
omitting details. Instead, composite figures and structures are
formed so that as little as possible is left out. As a result, dreams
often superimpose various words and ideas. This is most clearly
demonstrable in the way condensation treats words or names.
A thing with one name may be associated in a dream with an
event with a similar name, even though neither *word* occurred
in the dream. (Freud relates a case where a patient dreamed
that "*his uncle gave him a kiss in an automobile.* He went on at
once to give me the interpretation, which I myself would never
have guessed: namely that it meant 'auto-erotism'" [1900a:408-
409]).

In Abimelech's dream, condensation revolves around the
word *laqaḥ* ("take"). Abimelech condenses a set of images into
a single picture of the threatening deity who pronounces a
verdict of imminent death. Abimelech, like Pharaoh, had

"taken" Sarah. In fact, Abimelech *is* "a dead man" because of the woman he "took." But in this narrative the "taking" is a literal transporting of Sarah's person, not the usual euphemism for sexual relations. Unlike the incident in Genesis 12 where there can be little doubt that Pharaoh and Sarah had sex, in Genesis 20 nothing happens conjugally.[9] In fact, as Niditch notes, there is a "squeaky cleanness" (1987:57) attached to this "wife taking."

Characteristic of the primary-process of dream-work, in verse 3 Abimelech is unable to distinguish between reality and fiction, between his repressed wish for Sarah and actual sexual consummation. Since Abimelech "took" but did not "take," his dream can be seen as a representation of the fulfillment of his repressed desire for sexual relations with Sarah, to "take" her in *every* sense of the word.

The second activity in the primary-process of dream-work is *displacement*, which Freud regards as "the most powerful instrument of the dream-censorship" (1916-17:233). According to Freud, elements in the manifest dream (the "literal" contents of a dream as the dreamer remembers them) replace elements in the latent dream-thoughts (the "figurative" activity of a dream, the "forbidden" dream-thoughts) via a chain of associations in order to "disguise" these censored thoughts. As a result, the intensity of a repressed wish is detached from the wish itself and passes on to other thoughts which in themselves are of little value. Displacement in dreams is similar to the way jokes work in that a switch of context allows for a play on words. In both cases, however, the linkages may be forced and often far-fetched. (One such example is cited by Freud and concerns an upper-middle class male patient whose impending marriage to the daughter of a wealthy physician had just been called off. The young man dreamed he was climbing stairs, and Freud analyzed the dream as a displaced wish to "go up in the world" socially.)

In this case, Abimelech's unconscious wish is not revealed by the "manifest" text of the dream as such (God's threatening image), but rather by what Lacan calls "the lacunae latent within it" (1968:74). The king's dream is a product of his past and present that fantasizes his future, a *regression* in the service of a *progression*. That is, Abimelech's dream is not his *actual* unconscious wish, but rather a *distortion* of it. The most condensed content of Abimelech's dream (verse 3) goes piece by piece into his dream-story via a string of associations. In verses 4-7, the procedure is reversed during the "secondary-process" of dream-work. It is at this stage that Abimelech retraces his chain of associations in order to "decode" or interpret his dream.

THE SECONDARY-PROCESS OF DREAM WORK

This phase of dream-work takes place while the dreamer is beginning to awaken and attempts to return from the pictorial language of dreams to ordinary waking expressions, from fantasy to the introduction of a reality.

Since the conscious mind prefers to put the irrational dream-sequence into a recognizable and familiar logical order, the sequence of events is often taken "out of order." That is, during this stage, the dreamer reorganizes the "hieroglyphics," the pictorial dream images, into a relatively consistent and comprehensible narrative, filling in its gaps, smoothing over its contradictions, and reordering its chaotic elements. The "intelligible" pattern which the conscious mind wants to impose on the dream-images can ignore or falsify what is patently there (just like the reader Freud identifies who is so engaged in a text that he or she ignores the misprints [Freud 1900a:499]). What was visible to the mind's eye in the dream remains unchanged, but the conscious perspective produces a re-vision of it. The dream that one recalls is a transformation of an original dream (which itself is not the latent dream thought), never remembered exactly—only in re-vision. In this context, re-vision means to "see again" in two senses: to recall a dream and to generate a new narrative, to substitute a text for a text.

There is a close correspondence between reading and the secondary-process of dream-work. In both cases, "raw materials" are transformed in ways which must be analyzed, deciphered, and decomposed, and the focus is on "symptomatic" places in the text (distortions, ambiguities, absences, and elisions). Readers and dreamers continuously shift from metaphorical expressions to literal meanings, from repressed wishes to reality, and from indeterminate to determinate signifiers. Both readers and dreamers confer meaning to textual elements by allowing them to be successively displaced; both readers and dreamers revise personal dramas into scenarios of remembering, repeating, and working through.

Dream images, and what Holland refers to as "carbon black on dried wood pulp" (1975), are rendered into texts and contexts by reordering seemingly *arbitrary* contiguity to *meaningful* contiguity, parataxis to syntaxis. Opposing two competing strategies, readers and dreamers perceive symbols that enable an "authentic" image to be reconstructed from its distorting fragments.

At the same time, reading and dreaming give meaning to textual elements by allowing them to be successively displaced. The text (whether dream or literary) and its interpretation form a mirror-image: dreams and literary texts transform concepts (wishes or ideas) into symbolic images; dream interpretation and literary analysis travel the same road in reverse, from the semantic (the concept or idea) to the semiotic (the symbolic image used to represent the abstract thought).[10]

Of course, Freud and modern literary theorists are not the first to notice this interplay and apply it to biblical texts. Indeed, José Faur describes a similar relationship in the rabbinic tradition:

> . . . Scripture is expressive at both the semiotic and the semantic levels. The first level corresponds to *peshat*, the "literal" or "generally accepted" sense of Scripture. The other level corresponds to *derasha*—"interpretation"—the rabbinic method of Scriptural exegesis. The purpose of *peshat* is to expound the mind of the author as expressed in the text. The *derasha* interprets the text *independently* of the intention of the author. At this level, the elements of the text do not convey the meaning which they had at the semiotic level; the sense of the *derasha* is not the sum of the value of each of its components in isolation. As in all semantic compositions, the elements of the *derasha* acquire significance only through syntagmatic opposition, and are context-bound. "Every

exposition (*midrash-wu-midrash*) is context-bound," taught the rabbis. It is the text itself speaking to the reader. At this level there is no objective meaning: "One may not raise objections against an *aggada* [*derasha*]," said the rabbis. Interpretation is subjective: it is the creative composition of the reader functioning as author. (1986:122)

READING ABOUT DREAMS

Although the lure of all texts lies in the unveiling of the hidden, this is particularly evident in narratives *about* dreams, narratives which, by design, confuse readings and confound explanation. On the one hand, reading about dream images is particularly problematic since they, and the words used to describe them, are semantic. Thus, it is not only the narrative characters who are beset by illusion. On the other hand, in exploring the ground of images beyond what the text may *apparently* control, readers do find pleasure in the reversal of their own "great expectations," of seeing a hitherto unperceived figure, one "hidden in full view" (Lacan 1977:72).

If stories about dreams are generally enigmatic, biblical dreams seem to be even more so, since they force a reader to examine material which is of the "inherently covert mantological type" (Fishbane 1985:443). They are esoteric and require decoding. The representational status of what is "seen" must be clarified, despite the *seemingly* overt communication of God speaking directly.

Since dreams are semantic compositions, and given that the *derasha*-methodology is particularly suited to their interpretation, perhaps Freud intuitively applied rabbinic methodology to his interpretation of dreams! In any event, the rabbis, Freud, and many modern literary theorists[11] seem to be saying that the literary narrative and the dream are tales told *by* the unconscious *to* the conscious—in this case, Abimelech's *and* mine.

Although Abimelech is the narrative dreamer, I as a reader experience Abimelech's dream *and* my reading of it. As a reader, I must collaborate with Abimelech, supplying meaning where the text is indeterminate or discontinuous, where explanations are required to fill narrative elisions; and along with

Abimelech, a reader must open the text to comprehension, enlightening what is dark and obscure. As a reader, I must provide a correlation between Abimelech's semantic translation of the primary-process dream images of verse 3 and the secondary-process "explanation" of these images in verses 4-7, a correlation between Abimelech's fantasized past and an intrusion of his present "reality." That is, readers constantly re-vision.

However, since this is a narrative about a dream, a fiction-within-a-fiction, full of equivocations, reading about it signifies everything and nothing, veers further away from authenticity, employs distorted images which do not superficially correspond to what they represent, and undergoes transformations at every turn, in every new context, preventing a definitive reading. Due to intertextuality (see chapter 2, above), moreover, parallel texts combine with the interpretation of Abimelech's dream to focus attention on what I as reader know about earlier narrative events, "see" in the present text, and anticipate later in the story.

All of our knowledge about Abimelech, Abraham, and Sarah makes the death threat even more confusing. However, if we regard Gen 20:4-7 as the secondary-process of Abimelech's dream-work, these verses represent a response to Abimelech's repressed desire (discussed below), in both its distorted and actual forms.

REPRESSION

When Abimelech recalls his dream, the rationality of his daytime experiences imposes a narrative sense and coherence on the apparent absurdity of his dream-sequence. Thus, the ambiguity of the death threat may be explained by the Freudian concept of "repression."

Freud describes repression as the "preliminary stage of condemnation" (1915d:148). Certainly, Abimelech anticipates a condemnation which he apparently feels he deserves. This is indicated by the repeated use of the word "sin." In the dream discourse, the deity states that "It was I who withheld you from sinning against me" (Gen 20:6), and in Abimelech's subsequent rebuke to Abraham, the king uses this value-laden word twice: "How have I *sinned* against you, that you have brought upon me and upon my kingdom a great *sin*?" (Gen 20:9)

Equally significant is the use of "fear" in this passage. Abimelech's aides *"fear* greatly" when they hear of the king's dream (Gen 20:8). Abraham later says that he declared Sarah to be his sister because he felt "there is no *fear* of God in this place" (Gen 20:11). (Of course, Abraham's excuse takes on a certain irony: his "fear" serves rhetorically to emphasize Abimelech's fear.)

"Sin" and "fear"—the two words are redolent of the vocabulary of "guilt" (see chapter 4, below). And for Abimelech, as in Freudian theory, guilt anticipates condemnation and punishment. Indeed, the sequence—defensive words, threat of punishment, condemnation—fits Freud's paradigm (Freud 1905c:175). In Abimelech's dream, the threat of punishment by the deity is in response to Abimelech's repressed desire for Sarah, and is the intermediate stage between the king's defensive words and impending doom.

Andreas Resch explains the dream in Genesis 20 as Abimelech's inner psychological struggle; unconscious guilt assails him for having *taken* another man's wife (1964:20). Read this way, the narrative is not a dream story, but a madness story, a study of neurosis. I disagree. However systematically simplified the notion of repression is in this chapter, repression seems to be viewed by analysts in terms of intentionality, putting into question the notion of causality. For me as a reader, therefore, the question is: what are Abimelech's motives?

Dream interpretation is associated with power struggles, and this dream is no exception. A stranger comes to Gerar, and the local ruler, Abimelech, experiences sexual dysfunction. Clearly, on some level, there is a conflict between these two powerful men, and Abimelech seems to be losing. Reading only verse 3 as Abimelech's dream provides a coherent, rational explanation for his assorted dream imagery, as well as a justification for Abimelech's need for forgiveness. In other words, reading Gen 20:3 as the result of the primary-process of dream-work, and Gen 20:4-7 as the secondary-process, Abimelech's "fear" of condemnation and judgement can be understood, despite his seeming lack of "sin."

Although, for the most part, dreams are metaphorical, there are enough elements of reality in this dream for Abimelech to recognize the fact that Abraham is favored by God. The king is aware that only the morally questionable Abraham can act as intercessor and restore Abimelech's lost virility. Verses 4-7 verify Abimelech's "reading" of Abraham's status. Abimelech, the should-be "adversary" in Gen 20:1-18 is the victim (Niditch 1987:57).

DREAMS AS PROPHETIC

Twentieth-century psychology has been marked by tensions in connection with the dream text and its interpretation. Freud searches for the meaning of dreams in the past, as if to say that the dreamer's psyche interprets itself by exposing its underlying causes. Yet many post-Freudians, like the ancients, look beyond thoughts that may have inspired a dream toward future effects, shifting the focus from past causes to present conflicts and future possibilities. Although Freud discusses dreams as expressions of past wishes and not omens of future events, he does say that dreams and their interpretations may enter a cycle of self-fulfilling prophecy. In Freud's terminology, this is linked to the problem of suggestion. No dream in itself, but only an interpretation that has consequences for the dreamer's future, is prophetic. Perhaps this is the case for Abimelech.

Abimelech recognizes the power of Abraham. Abimelech never receives explicit reassurances from God who *openly* intervenes in Abraham's life. Abimelech's need for forgiveness emphasizes the king's recognition of Abraham as the principal instrument of power. Abimelech sees Abraham as the "prophet" who must intercede,[12] and, significantly, it is Abimelech who uses the word "prophet" in the Bible for the first time. Although this self-described "righteous nation" cannot comprehend the exact nature of the covenant between Abraham and his God, the foreign king's understanding of Abraham's *status* provides the needed forgiveness in no uncertain terms: Abraham "*will* pray for you and you *will* live" (Gen 20:7). But it is only *be-*

cause[13] Abraham will pray for Abimelech that the king and all that is his will live.

The irony, of course, is that Abimelech did nothing wrong. It was the duplicity of Abraham which caused the entire incident, and Abimelech knows this. As Abimelech interprets his dream, the predictive elements become dominant. Textually, Abimelech's dream is not simply a transformation of the narrative, a commentary on another level, but an integral part of it.

As a result, during the secondary-process of dream-work, when Abimelech is translating his dream into a coherent "scenario,"[14] he frees himself from the consequences of his repressed wishes by an almost classical example of the Freudian defense mechanism: rejection and disavowal. Freud's general description of this psychological process sounds as if it had been written specifically to describe the king of Gerar: ". . . [he] rejects the incompatible idea together with its effect and behaves as if the idea had never occurred to [him] at all" (1894a:58)! Abimelech "rejects the incompatible idea" (his desire for Sarah versus his fear of Abraham) "together with their effects" (Sarah as his, but also Abraham's wrath), and "behaves as if the idea had never occurred to him at all" (he does not *want* to sleep with Sarah; Sarah and Abraham tried to trick him into sleeping with her . . . "Lord! Even a righteous nation will you slay?").

INTERPRETING THE INTERPRETER

As Freud pointed out, dream texts receive meaning retrospectively, and Abimelech's is no exception. It is the status of words and signs which is at issue. In looking back on the narrative from the closural vantage point, details, like dream images, assume new shape and meaning. The king gives Abraham a complete choice of where to settle in addition to sheep, oxen, and male and female slaves.[15] Abimelech then speaks to Sarah (20:16), and his words are very ambiguous:

> Look! I have given your "brother" a thousand pieces of silver. Look here! It is an "eye-covering"—to you and to all who are with you. To all you are . . . "vindicated" [*wenokahat*].

Some traditional commentators claim that Abimelech is instructing Sarah not to appear in public with an uncovered face so that her beauty will not be a temptation to other men (Sarna 1989:144). Others interpret this verse figuratively, that is, Sarah's honor was not violated, and so Abimelech is making a payment to "cover the eyes" of everyone to protect himself from scorn.[16]

I read this sentence differently. Abimelech's words drip with sarcasm. Although the root y-k-h ("vindicate") is used often in the context of "giving judgement" in a neutral or even positive light (see, e.g., Gen 24:14, 44), there are many places in the Hebrew Bible where "rebuke" would be a more appropriate translation (e.g., Gen 31:42). In a nice play on words, by telling Sarah "you have been . . . vindicated," Abimelech simultaneously "rebukes" Sarah:

> Look! I have given your "brother" a thousand pieces of silver.
> Look here! It is an "eye-covering"—to you and to all who are with you. To all you are . . . "rebuked." (Gen 20:16)

Of course, interpretation does not stop with the story itself. *Reading* the text represents a continuation of Abimelech's hermeneutical process. Just as I as reader become Abimelech's double as he tries to make sense of his dream, I also experience Abimelech's skepticism about Abraham while striving, as Harold Fisch states, to "make sense of the story" (1984:50).

As Holland observes (1975), individual reading responses disclose essential psychological characteristics; that is, readers "use" literature to rediscover themselves through "transactions" with texts. Each reader and each dreamer, in interpreting a text, makes it his or her own.[17] Meaning does not lie inside the text or the psyche; what is supposedly *inside* depends upon what is *beyond* it. Dream interpretation and reading rely on basic opposition: manifest and latent dream contents, dream images and concealed meanings, explicit and implicit layers, surface and depth structures. Texts—dream and literary—are multiple, mutable, personal, and historical.

For me, reading Genesis 20 moves the Abraham-Sarah saga on to a new meaning, undermining its old power and deriving new power by exposing its major contradictions. Abraham is neither inside nor out, neither wholly king nor wholly servant, a husband who is no husband, a brother who is no brother, a picaresque character who, having played this game before, succeeded in gaining greater wealth from Pharaoh by pandering. Yet he is favored by the deity. Abimelech struggles with this issue; as a reader, so do I.

On one level, there is no distinction between Abimelech and myself. Trying to make sense of the dream implicates us both; we are caught in the net of signs. But the earlier scene of disguise and false recognition in Genesis 12 (discussed in chapter 2, above) reverberates, and its meaning is both cognitive and performative. Abimelech's dream sets the stage and enacts a narrative, but I as reader produce further texts. From the interpretation of Abimelech's dream and my dream of interpretation there is no escape. In a world permeated by deceit, only Abimelech sees beyond appearances. Abimelech "rebukes" Abraham and "vindicates" himself. His readers can do more and no less.

4

DAUGHTERS AND FATHERS
IN GENESIS,
OR,
WHAT IS WRONG
WITH THIS PICTURE?

Come to me, my child. Let me embrace the body I never
thought to touch again.

—Sophocles, *Oedipus at Colonus*

t is not surprising that biblical narratives depict a definable
family structure. What *is* surprising, however, is the conspicuous
absence of a figure lurking beneath the text, a figure repeatedly
subjected to erasure, exclusion, and transformation. Genesis
lacks daughters. Narrative after narrative describes the desire for
male children, the lengths to which women would go to have
sons, and the great joy surrounding the birth of a boy. Indeed,
of the possible structural permutations of parent-child relationships, the father and son pair is the one most frequently in
focus, and the mother and son is second. Mother-daughter and
father-daughter pairs receive the least narrative attention and
reflect a hierarchy of value that isolates the daughter as the
most absent member of the family institution.

Since the daughter's presence is normal and necessary to
the biological realities of family, and given the relevance of the
daughter as the figure upon whose mobility the entire kinship
structure rests, her narrative absence is significant and calls
attention to itself. I contend, therefore, that beneath the surface

father-son narration, the daughter-father relationship lies suppressed.

My purpose in exploring the scarcity of daughters in Genesis is not to generate a catalogue of exclusions. Indeed, perhaps because I cannot help but think that Genesis contains something more fraught with ambivalence than a narration of disinterested fathers, I read daughters in a more paradoxical way. Instead of measuring what the daughter may or may not materially contribute to the family, I wish to consider how she threatens it.

The most obvious answer, of course, is that while yet within her father's house, the daughter is the only member of the family who does not participate in extending the patronymic line. But that answer is too superficial. By reading Genesis simultaneously with Freud, the narrative erasure of biblical daughters can be seen as a parallel of Freud's rejection of the seduction-theory of hysteria (which I discuss below). A subtext emerges which necessitates silencing the daughter: What makes the nearly absent daughter so central in this otherwise emphatically masculine epic is her potential to determine and expose a threat to the father's power and patriarchal rule. At the deepest layer of biblical narrative, the (unacknowledged) daughter is the structural catalyst who enables yet endangers patriarchy. By consequence, she is also the figure who problematizes the text and hence gets erased from it.

THE "ABSENT" DAUGHTER

The fact that father and son are homologous needs little illustration: It is the central presumption upon which Hebrew Scriptures depends, and it constitutes the basis for patrilineage. (Crucial to this chapter, it is also the central metaphor in which psychoanalytic theory is grounded.) Throughout the biblical text, a son is regarded as a special blessing, more often than not the direct result of divine intervention in a couple's life. So important are sons that barren women sometimes resort to having children by their handmaids (Gen 16:2; 30:3).[1]

The birth of a daughter, on the other hand, by no means creates such attention. Instead, there is a certain bland indifference to her narrative presence. As Leonie Archer notes, biblical genealogical tables "indicate a startling disparity in the ratio of male:female births, a disparity which can in no way reflect a demographic reality" (1990:18). The tables do, however, reflect the attitude towards daughters. Inscribed within Genesis is something more than a general disregard of women; the *daughter* is specifically absent.

To consider the daughter and father in relation to each other is to juxtapose the two most asymmetrical figures in terms of gender, age, authority, and privilege. The daughter, the liminal or "threshold" person in the family, symbolically stands at the boundary-door, blocked from departure by the father. Even their narrative locations construct polarities. In fact, a repeated theme in biblical narratives is a daughter's transgression against her father and subsequent departure from the closure of his house. For example, Dinah "goes out," is raped (Gen 34:1-2), and is then narratively banished from the text (Rashkow 1990:98-100). Similarly, the departure of Jephthah's daughter from her father's house is viewed by Jephthah as a transgression *against him* ("Alas, my daughter! *You* have brought me very low, and *you* have become the cause of trouble to me" [Judg 11:35]). Jephthah, who has returned from a battle a victor, is nevertheless felled like a defeated warrior by his daughter, emphasized by his word choice: *kara'* is used most often in the context of soldiers killed in war (as in Judg 5:27; 2 Sam 22:40; Isa 46:1-2; 65:12; Pss 18:40; 20:9; 72:9; 78:31).

What the biblical text seems to privilege at the expense of all else is the patriarchal prerogative to retain daughters. The biblical daughter out of her "correct" locale becomes a threat. Therefore, although the daughter is excluded from the patrilineal and patronymic significance of the family house, she is to remain imprisoned within it. When daughters such as Dinah or Jephthah's daughter (who is left unnamed) cross over the threshold of their father's house, they enter a tacitly forbidden zone where female presence impugns the family honor. Hebrew Scripture in effect becomes a "code" for what is subliminally the father's story of the sins of the daughter, as Jephthah's words to his daughter indicate. Decoded, the father's accusations might read that *because of* the sins of the daughter, daughters leave the protective enclosure and become maternal figures. Daughters are subsumed as mothers, and the text "reads itself through a chain-male linkage" (Boose 1989:22). Even when her identity as daughter is exchanged for wife, however, she is still the alien until she has once again changed her sign to "mother of new members of the lineage," which by implication means mother to a son.

INCEST

As I discuss below, these repeated biblical narratives of a daughter's "transgression" seem to be prototypical of Freud's narrative of the "catastrophe" that leaves "the path to the development of femininity . . . open to the girl" (Freud 1925j:241). Significantly, the "catastrophe" Freud describes is father-daughter incest. If read from that perspective, the biblical daughter can be seen as locked into a conflicted text of desire and prohibition.

Lévi-Strauss's well-known analysis of kinship systems argues that the most significant rule governing any family structure is the ubiquitous existence of the incest taboo which imposes the social aim of exogamy and alliance upon the biological events of sex and procreation. Indeed, Genesis nearly constitutes a meditation on the questions which concern where wives for the patriarchy should come from, how closely they should be related to "us," or how "other" they should be (Pitt-Rivers 1977:128, 165). Yet within the patriarchal sagas, Abraham twice acknowledges his wife to be his sister, and his son, Isaac marries his father's-brother's-daughter.[2] Isaac's son, Jacob, acquires two wives, sisters who constitute a lineal double of each other. That is, Jacob marries two of his father's-father's-brother's-son's-son's-daughters, who are simultaneously his mother's-brother's-daughters and thus again are connected back to Abraham. In the next generation, Reuben sleeps with his father's-second-wife's-maid, symbolically violating family purity laws, and Judah sleeps with his daughter-in-law.[3] The list is quite impressive: Adam-Eve, Noah-Ham, Lot-his daughters, Reuben-Bilhah, and Jacob-Tamar all involve parent-child incestuous congress or exposure, while Adam-Eve and Abraham-Sarah are brother-sister unions (as is Amnon-Tamar in 2 Sam), and Isaac-Rebekah and Jacob-Leah-Rachel are cousin marriages. Is there a pattern here? Contra Lévi-Strauss, familial and sexual integrity across Genesis seem to be observed more in the breach than in the maintenance. Why?

GUILT VERSUS SHAME

While many elements of the conventional vocabulary of moral deliberation (such as "ethical," "virtuous," "righteous," and their opposites) are largely alien to the psychoanalytic lexicon, the concepts of "guilt" and "shame" do appear, albeit in technical (and essentially nonmoral) contexts (Smith 1986:52). "Guilt" and "shame" are described as different emotional responses, stemming from different stimuli, reflecting different patterns of behavior, and functioning in different social constructions (although the two are often related). Their primary distinction lies in the norm that is violated and the expected consequences.

Guilt relates to internalized, societal and parental *prohibitions*, the transgression of which creates feelings of wrong-doing and the fear of punishment (Piers and Singer 1953).

Shame, on the other hand, relates to the anxiety caused by "inadequacy" or "failure" to live up to internalized societal and parental *goals and ideals* (as opposed to internalized prohibitions), expectations of what a person "should" do, be, know, or feel. These feelings of failure often lead to a fear of psychological or physical rejection, abandonment, expulsion (separation anxiety), or loss of social position (Alexander 1948:43).[4] One often feels the need to avenge his or her humiliation, to "save face." By "shaming the shamer," the situation is reversed, and the shamed person feels triumphant (Horney 1950:103).

The difference between guilt and shame is subtle, but important in the context of this chapter. Within the biblical text, "shame" is a powerful and prevalent emotion and sanction, as is indicated by the preponderance of Hebrew words used to convey the violation of goals and ideals. The differences in meaning among these words are often hard to discern in translation,[5] but the main oppositional term to shame is the root k-b-d used for both "honor" and "heaviness": honor increases "heavy" esteem, while shame decreases it, causing "light" esteem. "Shame" words are often accompanied by phrases that express "shame on the face" (blushing), shame expressed in body position (hanging the head), or a reduction in social position in his/her own eyes and in the eyes of others (e.g., Jer 48:39; 2 Sam 10:5; Isa 16:14; Jer 50:12).

Strikingly, the vocabulary for "guilt" is far less extensive than that for "shame."[6] Based on sheer volume alone, it would appear that the text is less concerned with the violation of societal prohibitions, in this case, incest, than the failure to achieve internalized goals, that is, the idealization and perpetuation of patriarchy and family prestige.

It is within this framework that the father-daughter relationship becomes problematic, complex in ways that even the mother-son dynamic is not, despite the same asymmetries of age, authority, and gender-privilege that work to separate mother and son. On the one hand, daughters are property belonging exclusively to the father. Since it is the father who controls the exchange of women, the woman most practically available to be exchanged is not the mother, who sexually belongs to her father, nor the sister, who comes under the bestowal rights of her own father, but the daughter (thus, Leah and Rachel, Laban's daughters, are bartered for economic profit in Genesis 29).[7] And as the Genesis 34 narrative of Jacob's daughter Dinah makes clear, rape is not considered a violation of the daughter so much as a theft of property that deprives her father and necessitates compensation to him.

On the other hand, although the daughter is clearly regarded as legal property inside the family, she is not a commodity to be bartered in the same way as an ox or an ass. She is explicitly sexual property, acquired by the father's sexual expenditure and his own family bloodline, not by economic transaction. Her presence as daughter highlights the sexual aspect within the family configuration and necessitates a detailed taboo, codified in Leviticus 18, which ostensibly defines illicit congress. Virtually every family female (mother, sister,[8] aunt,[9] cousin, sister-in-law, niece, daughter-in-law, granddaughter, and so on[10]) is off-limits. Conspicuously, the only one not included is the daughter. Of all possible forms of incest, therefore, that between father and daughter is overlooked. As Judith Herman and Lisa Hirschman point out,

> The wording of the law makes it clear that . . . what is prohib-ited is the sexual use of those women who, in one manner or another, already belong to other relatives. Every man is thus expressly forbidden to take the daughters of his kinsmen, but only by implication is he forbidden to take his own daughters. (1981:61)

Although the incest prohibitions demarcate male territory, first and foremost of their concerns is to avoid curtailing the desires (and the sexual control) of the father. Thus, the daughter's presence within the father's house retains, figurative-ly if not literally, an incestuous option that implicitly threatens to pollute the family structure.[11]

Since the text lacks the father-daughter taboo, the father-daughter relationship has no internalized prohibitions (hence no "guilt"). But the purity of a wife is the law of first priority upon which patrilineage depends. The daughter may be carrying the father's seed. Since the father is the one who has had exclusive control of the daughter's sexuality until the point of marriage, it is at the juncture of the daughter's marriage (and transfer of proprietary rights from father to son-in-law) that father-daughter incest becomes problematic. Evidence of lack of virginity would cause the son-in-law to point a finger directly at the character whom the text privileges, the one status role which the narrative repeatedly goes out of its way to exempt from blame of any sort: the father. The biblical daughter becomes dangerous to the father's authority, and her existence within the "safety" of her family ambivalent.

THE ACCUSED BRIDE

It is in this context that the elaborately detailed punishment for the accused bride in Deut 22:13-21 makes sense.

In the three sex laws that follow this one in chapter 22, the father is either unmentioned or minimally important. If, for instance, a man forcibly seizes an unbetrothed virgin and "they are found," he must pay her father fifty shekels and marry her (22:28-29). If a man lies with a betrothed virgin inside the city, the two offenders are to be taken outside the gate of the town and stoned to death, she for not "crying out" and he for "violating the wife of his neighbor." The father is not involved here, but the male violator (as well as the female property that is now "soiled") must die, since the future rights of another man have been stolen.[12]

All of the numerous proscriptions codified in Deuteronomy are essentially purification laws to "banish evil from Israel." Deut 22:13-21, however, is unique in that it thrusts the father to the very center of the drama and makes him a special actor, *protected* by a formulaic dialogue, yet placed into the role of *defendant* against the son-in-law's charges of the daughter's impurity.

Implicitly, the husband has accused the man who gave him this woman of having taken the husband's property (her virginity) in advance. If evidence of virginity exists, the groom is flogged and must pay the father one-hundred shekels "for publicly defaming a virgin of Israel." But the payment is made to the father, so perhaps we should read "for publicly defaming a virgin's *father*." If the bride's virginity cannot be substantiated,

> They shall take her to the door of her father's house and her fellow citizens shall stone her to death for having committed an infamy in Israel by disgracing her father's house. (Deut 22:21)

This crime is not merely "an evil" to be "banished from the midst." It is "an infamy in Israel" that disgraces the father's house (the place from which the punishment implies it emanated) by tacitly accusing him of incest. However, by transposing cause and effect the father's reputation is protected. That is, because no hymeneal blood was shed in her husband's house the daughter's blood is to be shed on her father's door. A threat to the father's reputation (and hence his power) is averted by deflecting blame for sexual misconduct, real or imagined, from the privileged patriarch onto the powerless daughter. Consistent with the patterns described by Horney (above), the "shamed thus shames the shamer."

Silently, however, the punishment exposes an underlying syntax; that is, by inference it marks the house as the location where the violation occurred. As such, it can be argued that the relations of biblical daughters and fathers can resemble in some important ways the model developed by Herman and Hirschman to describe the family situations of contemporary incest victims: a dominating, authoritarian father; an absent, ill, or complicitous mother; and a daughter who, prohibited from speaking about the abuse, is unable to reconcile her contradictory feelings of love for her father and terror of him, her desire to end the abuse, and her fear that if she speaks out she will destroy the family structure that is her only security (Herman and Hirschman 1981, esp. chaps. 1, 4-7).

FREUD'S ABANDONMENT OF THE SEDUCTION THEORY

A parallel construct exists in Freud's abandonment of his seduction theory. When Freud first began working with hysterical patients, in every case he found an account of childhood sexual abuse by a member of the patient's own family, and it was almost always the father.[13] On this evidence, Freud developed his "seduction theory," that is, hysterical symptoms have their origin in sexual abuse suffered in childhood which is repressed and eventually assimilated to later sexual experience. Within a year, however, Freud wrote that he "no longer believe[d] in neurotica" (these psychosomatic symptoms resulting from childhood sexual abuse; in Froula 1989:118). At this point, Freud founded psychoanalytic theory upon the Oedipus complex.

This change was crucial. Anna Freud wrote that "keeping up the seduction theory would mean abandoning the Oedipus complex, and with it the whole importance of fantasy life. . . . In fact, I think there would have been no psychoanalysis afterwards" (in Masson 1983:113). A more critical reading of Freud's abandonment of his seduction theory has emerged in feminist scholarship over the last decade. As several critics have argued, Freud turned away from the seduction theory because he was unable to come to terms with his discovery, which was the abuse of paternal power.[14] The cases of Anna O., Lucy R., Katharina, Elisabeth von R., and Rosalia H. described in *Studies on Hysteria* (Freud and Breuer 1895d) all connect symptoms with fathers or, in Lucy's case, with a father substitute (in two cases Freud misrepresents the father as an uncle). His reluctance to implicate the father appears in a supplemental narrative of an unnamed patient whose physician-father accompanied her during sessions with Freud. When Freud challenged her to acknowledge that "something else had happened which she had not mentioned," she "gave way to the extent of letting fall a single significant phrase; but she had hardly said a word before she stopped, and her old father, who was sitting behind her, began to sob bitterly." Freud concludes: "Naturally I pressed my investigation no further; but I never saw the patient again" (Freud and Breuer 1895d:100-101). The issue for Freud was credit versus authority: Whose story is one to believe, the father's or the daughter's?

The list of reasons Freud gives for abandoning the seduction theory is not very compelling; indeed, it contradicts his own evidence in *Studies on Hysteria*. Freud complains that he cannot terminate the analyses, although he describes several cases (notably Anna O./Bertha Pappenheim) as "terminating in a lasting cure." He complains of not being able to distinguish between truth and "emotionally charged fiction" in his patients, yet he links the vanishing of their symptoms with the recovery of traumatic experience through memory (narrated with apparent fidelity to literal fact in Katharina's case, and in dream imagery by Anna O. [Freud and Breuer 1895d:43]). Nevertheless, for a number of reasons (the fact that the fathers, not the daughters, paid him being only the most obvious), Freud acceded to the father's text. The problem was precisely that sexual abuse of children by fathers appeared "so general." Not only did Freud uncover it within the bounds of the hysterics' private and individual histories. During the years between conceiving and abandoning the seduction theory, Freud was engaged in self-analysis, and he discovered, through dreams, his own incestuous wishes towards his daughter Mathilde and, through symptoms exhibited by his siblings, the possibility that his father Jakob had abused his children. Freud writes:

> . . . the astonishing thing that in every case *my own not excluded*, blame was laid on perverse acts by the father, and realization of the unexpected frequency of hysteria, in every case of which the same thing applied, though it was hardly credible that perverted acts against children were so general. (in Froula 1989:119)

In addition, Freud faced implications that would have changed the focus of his work from individual therapy to social criticism. The "icy reception" with which the professional community of *fin de siècle* Vienna greeted his 1896 lecture, which did not even explicitly implicate fathers in hysteria, seemed indication enough that Freud, if he credited the daughters, would risk sharing their fate of being silenced and ignored (Schur 1972:104).

While many analysts have simply followed Freud in rejecting the seduction theory for the Oedipal theory, others have tried to explain and resolve the apparently contradictory ideas of "seduction-as-fact" and "seduction-as-fantasy" by means of Freud's concepts of "*psychic* reality" and "*primal* fantasy." [15] That is, seduction can be a *representation* of the father's repressed and deflected sexual desires, or even a metaphor for power ("primal fantasy"). Since *actual* incest need not occur, the gap between the "real" and the "imaginary," the very structure of fantasy, is bridged.

THE FIRST FATHER-DAUGHTER "SEDUCTION"

Conveniently, this brings us to the creation narrative in Genesis 1-3, and the first daughter. While almost all interpretations of this text acknowledge its sexual nature, traditional exegesis has concentrated on "Adam's Fall." But the familiar story masks two interwoven subtexts: Freud's sexualized father-daughter narrative in which the Adam material appears merely as a re-narration, and a feminist narrative of an unacknowledged daughter's rebellion by means of her appropriating the forbidden fruit that stands "erected" at the center of the enclosed garden.

Read from this perspective, the first subtext emerges. The father has planted an invitation to transgress (a metaphoric seduction) accompanied by a prohibition against doing so. The ambivalence of the father's part in the "Fall," which has been the focus of considerable theological commentary, perhaps can be seen as Freud's "catastrophe," with its dangerous potential inherent in the daughter's "transition to the father object" (Freud 1925j:241). The father desires yet forbids desiring; he simultaneously wants but does not want the transgression he has provoked, a transgression he will deny and punish. This ambivalence is textually revealed by its most psychologically accurate defense. Just as Freud, by abandoning the seduction theory, deflects guilt from the father to (variously) the nurse, the mother,[16] and, by way of the Oedipus complex, the child herself, so the biblical father projects his seduction onto others and thus denies paternal complicity.

The seduction is displaced first onto the (phallic) serpent. The indicator I see for the serpent's phallic symbolism is based less on the obvious Freudian association of shape than on two other factors. First, since Hebrew has no neuter gender, nouns must be either masculine or feminine and the word for serpent (*nahash*) is, indeed, masculine. Second, the narrative function of the serpent, and his description as "the most wily of the beasts of the field which YHWH had made" (Gen 3:1), anticipates, and seems embedded in, Augustine's famous use of the "Fall" to explain the frustrating unruliness of the male sexual organ.

The serpent as seducer thus established, blame is then displaced onto the daughter herself in her seduction of Adam. The chain of deflections to protect the father begins. It is not the father but the serpent who seduces the daughter and, by the end of this narrative, it is the daughter who seduces Adam, her "father"! Paradigmatically, the "shamed shames the shamer." To effect this, however, the narrative subjects itself to a labyrinth of self-exposing transformations.

Some feminist biblical scholars see Genesis 1 as a mitigating authorization for women's equality.[17] I disagree. Every authorization of equality in Genesis 1 is subsequently repressed and erased by chapters 2-3. In fact, the juxtaposition of the two accounts of creation exposes the shadowed family construct and highlights the subtext of deflected paternal desire.

The syntax in Gen 1:26-27, which implies man and woman are created simultaneously and equally,[18] constructs Adam and Eve as son and daughter. Typical of the defense mechanism associated with projection and denial, this narration attempts to reconstitute the family into a desired model. This, however, makes the deity overtly a father who authorizes his children's implicitly incestuous union (i.e., brother-sister incest), and therefore necessitates a re-narration which erases and excludes his role.

When chapter 2 re-creates man and woman, it omits the parallelism of the chapter 1 account and disassociates the deity entirely from the parentage of the woman, further distancing the original father-daughter relationship. Simultaneously, it removes the incestuous implications of the brother-sister union by eliminating the license given in chapter 1 for the human children to be fruitful and eat of all the "trees with seed bearing fruit" without restriction. Adam's paternal parentage remains, and even his maternal parent is implicitly present in the earth from which he is shaped, but Eve, who is born from Adam's body has a lineage lost in ambiguities.[19]

No matter how her creation is read, what seems clear is that the text has tried to detach her genealogy from the father and place it with Adam. Ironically, however, in an attempt to mask the threat of deflected desire, the text inadvertently reconstitutes it. Because of the emphasis placed on Eve's derivation from Adam's side, and therefore Adam's implied paternity, the narrative reinforces the paradigm of a tacitly condoned but overtly disclaimed act between father and daughter. The original father-daughter story, which has been so problematic, is repressed but remains visible in Adam. Adam, the acknowledged son, becomes the father, making father and son analogous (and as Boose points out, this relationship is then changed in Christianity to synonymous [1989:48]).

THE DAUGHTER'S REBELLION AGAINST THE FATHER

At the same time, the text also contains the subtext of Eve's appropriation of the forbidden fruit, a mythology of the daughter's rebellion into sexual maturity, a "seizing" of her fruitfulness.

In replacing his seduction theory with the Oedipus complex, Freud explains that a daughter's attachment to her father parallels a son's attachment to his mother; but for the girl, attachment to the father is "positive," following an earlier "negative" phase in which she learns that her mother has not "given" her a penis. She turns in despair to the father, who may be able to give her some of its power (Freud 1925j and 1931b *et passim*).[20] If read from Freud's perspective, the "seed-bearing fruit" on the father's tree might signify the father's self, the "father's Phallus" in both its Lacanian meaning as a symbol of paternal authority[21] and its Freudian significance as the physical sign of "presence" and biological superiority. The taboo on plucking/eating this knowledge of good and evil forbids Eve, the daughter, from obtaining the father's potency and privilege.

This symbolism becomes clearer if we follow the time-honored exegetical practice of reading the Bible intertextually (on which, see Fewell 1992). Just before the children of Israel are to enter the Promised Land, which is a recapitulation of "the Father's original garden" (Frye 1982:72), the fruit taboo resurfaces and with it, its phallic significance:

> When you enter the land and plant all [manner of] trees for food, you will regard its fruits as *uncircumcised*. For three years it will be to you a thing *uncircumcised*, and it *will not be eaten*. (Lev 19:23)

Placed into this context, Genesis 3 seems to narrate the daughter's desire to acquire the father's knowledge and power through the (phallic) sign that has been denied her, and dramatizes the threat to patriarchy which daughters represent. By asserting her desire for the sign that confers exclusive rights to the male, the daughter symbolically challenges the privilege of the gender system signified by the Phallus.

The text, confronted with a daughter's desires which have no legitimate place in its patriarchal order, mutes them by denial and displacement. By reasserting the primacy of the father-son relationship, the story represses the more threatening material of its father-daughter subtext.[22] Thus, Eve gives the "seed-bearing fruit" to Adam and becomes the medium through which this symbol of potency and privilege (the Phallus in both Freudian and Lacanian meanings) is passed from father to son. Simultaneously, Eve fulfills the mother's role inside the biblical nuclear family: first, to enable the reproductive linkage between father and son, and afterwards to mediate it.

Once Eve has transferred the fruit to Adam's possession, she transfers also her narrative centrality. Eve as *daughter* disappears into the margins of the story. Eve as *mother* effectively banishes the female transgressor of the father's garden. Her denied desires are perpetuated into a frustrated "yearning," what Freud might have called "penis envy" or the daughter's "recognition of absence." Read from this perspective, the iconographical moments of the garden and the "Fall" sequentially recapitulate the story of the pre-Oedipal state of "ignorance" and the "knowledge" obtained by psychosexual development.

But it is also a recognition of what Freud's feminist interpreters have defined as another kind of knowledge, the knowledge of the way "cultural stereotypes have been mapped onto the genitals" (Rubin 1975:195). If in the "phallic phase," as Freud asserts, "only one kind of genital organ comes to account—the male" (1923e:142), then Eve's act of aggression may be understood as a representation of her desire to get beyond the prohibitiveness of the Phallus and its rule as standard, what Luce Irigaray calls "the reign of the One, of Unicity" (1977:43), of the Father.

Eve's choice to give fruit, the conventional symbol of female sexuality, to another male may represent the daughter's ultimate dispossession of her father, and may thus reveal the daughter as *the* dangerous threat to paternal power, the reason for narrative absence. The daughter's act is a violation cursed by the father and results in a permanent barrier of separation. At the daughter's instigation, the son has cast aside perpetual security. This represents an outright rejection of the father and his authority. That is, *because of* the sins of the daughter, sons leave their father's control ("This is why a man leaves his father" [Gen

2:24]).[23] It is at this junction that the two interwoven sub-texts merge.

The original commandment to be fruitful and multiply is transformed into the structures of taboo, transgression, and punishment. Adam is now a laborer, and Eve is ordered into the *creation* of family, her presence as daughter permanently eliminated. Significantly, from now on (with the exception of the anomalous story of Ibzan in Judg 12:9), biblical fathers assiduously avoid ever giving daughters away. In fact, the Hebrew Bible avoids daughters almost altogether once the "collective catastrophe" of Gen 6:4, brought about by the generic "*daughters* of men," occurs. In that odd (and obscure) fragment, the "sons of God" are seduced by desire for the "daughters of men." The corrupt offspring produced by this union is one motive for God's decision to destroy humanity by the flood. In the Apocrypha, the union is said to defile the immortal sons but not the hapless daughters. This early elaboration of the "daughters of men" narrative begins a long tradition of attributing the origin of evil: here, as elsewhere, the problem revolves around women positionally coded as "daughters."

LOT AND HIS DAUGHTERS

A father and daughter do, however, re-enter the biblical narrative with the tale of Lot (Genesis 19), which intervenes between the Abram-Sarai stories of Genesis 12 and 20 (discussed in chapters 2 and 3, above). Until Lot, no biblical father is reported to have begotten a first-born daughter, and not one of the most important fathers (Adam, Noah, Abraham) is recorded as ever having any daughters at all. Lot destroys this impressive record by becoming the first father to produce no sons. Perhaps as a result, this story is an exemplum of the perils of biblical daughterhood.

Genesis 19 relates that two angels in (male) human form come as visitors to Lot's house in Sodom. Lot makes a lavish feast for them and invites them to stay overnight.[24] The wicked men of Sodom, young and old, surround the house and demand that he surrender the "men" to them. The details of this scene are chilling:

> Before they lay down, the men of the city, the men of Sodom,
> surrounded the house—from young to old, all the people,
> entirely. (19:4)

The narrator emphatically emphasizes the number and strength
of the mob: the *entire* male populace demands to sexually
brutalize the visitors. They shout "Bring them out to us that we
may know them" (Gen 19:5).

Lot's response is strange and shrouded in secrecy. The
narrator describes how he departs deliberately from the protection of his house ("Lot went out of the entrance-way to the
men, and shut the door after him"), in order to present his
alternative in secret, rather than eliciting the assistance of the
angels in thwarting the plan of the townsmen. Lot's alternative
is violent—that his daughters be raped instead:

> "Please, my brothers, do not so wickedly. Look, I have two
> daughters who have not known man. Please, I shall bring
> them out to you. Do to them as is good in your eyes. Only to
> these men do nothing because they came under the shadow
> of my roof." (Gen 19:7-8)

Lot speaks to the men of the town as though they were
comrades, addressing them as "brothers" (19:7). Inexplicably,
even though Lot recognizes that their proposal is evil, he tries to
substitute an equally violent act. The men of Sodom want the
angels, but Lot offers his daughters who, he stresses, have not
"known man," their virginity being a necessary aspect to the
last part of the narrative. Indeed, Lot *volunteers* to hand them
over to be abused by the crowd. Since the daughters are betrothed (19:14), and since the rape of a betrothed woman is a
crime punishable by death (Deut 22:23-27), Lot's actions could
have implicated him as an accomplice. Were these actions a
simple strategy to protect the angels, or were they an accurate
precursor to the incest Lot actually commits at the end of the
chapter?

Lot's offer to the mob is incredible! Or is it? In the account
of Lot's daughters, the narrator's explicit views about the
potential violence to them are not directly revealed; nevertheless, the narrative itself presents a powerful portrait of the
effects of threatened sexual violence. Most commentators

recognize that the proposed sodomy against the (male) angels is portrayed as reprehensible, yet they have been rather sympathetic to Lot's actions toward his daughters. Instead of condemning the offer of his daughters as rape victims, they point to the "mitigating circumstances," the demands of "hospitality," which excuse his behavior. John Calvin, for example, writes that "Lot's great virtue was sprinkled with some imperfection . . . Although he does not hesitate to prostitute his daughters . . . Lot, indeed is urged by extreme necessity" (in Lerner 1986:172).

Modern commentators have essentially followed this line of reasoning, and their pro-Lot position is illustrated by this statement of Bruce Vawter:

> Certainly to our tastes he [Lot] proves himself to be more sensitive to the duties of hospitality than those of fatherhood . . . the spectacle of a father offering his virgin daughters to the will and pleasure of a mob that was seeking to despoil his household would not have seemed as shocking to the ancient sense of proprieties as it may seem to us. . . . Really, there is no need to make excuses for him, as far as the biblical perspective is concerned. In all the stories about him the soundness of Lot's judgement is never the point at issue. . . . He is a good and not a bad man. (1977:235-236)

Skinner's assessment of Lot's character is similar. He states, "Lot's readiness to sacrifice the honour of his daughters . . . shows him as a courageous champion of the obligations of hospitality in a situation of extreme embarrassment, and is recorded to his credit" (1930:307). So, too, Sarna, who comments that "Lot is true to his code of honor. Hospitality was a sacred duty, according the guest the right of asylum" (1989:135). Surprisingly, Speiser, who otherwise annotates Genesis line by line, has no comment here. His only hint of a gloss on the incident with the daughters is this sentence: "True to the unwritten code, Lot will stop at nothing in his effort to protect his guests" (1964:123). Lest I be accused of viewing these readings as cases of literary mal[e]-practice, Nehama Leibowitz's comments are as favorable towards Lot as the male exegetes quoted above: "Lot tried to maintain Abraham's way of life [!] even in the heart of Sodom striving to preserve, at the risk to his life [?], the elementary obligations of hospitality to strangers . . . resulting in his throwing his daughters to the mercy of the populace, in exchange for his guests" (1981:176).

Although Niditch correctly points out that the potential rape of the divine messengers is "a doubly potent symbol of a cultural, non-civilized behavior from the Israelite point of view" (1982:369), what about the threat of sexual brutality to the daughters? Why would this not be equally reprehensible in the Israelite perspective? Could it be possible that the narrator believes that Lot's behavior is excusable? It appears so. This narrative declares that all socially approved actions and societal values must be subordinated to the "higher" obligations of hospitality, but only to male guests (as the brutal story of Judges 19 further illustrates).[25] Apparently, Lot's right to dispose of his daughters, even so as to offer them to be raped, is taken for granted. It does not need to be explained.[26] Once again, the male protector, either husband (as in the case of Abraham in Genesis 12 and 20) or the father (as in Lot's case) becomes the procurer.[27]

In an interesting reversal, Lot is saved by the angels. The mob storms the house and is about to break the door when the angels strike blind all the men of Sodom, warn Lot of the imminent destruction of the city, and prophetically tell him that he and his "family" will be saved.[28]

At this point, the narrative needs an available Eve to pluck fruit and offer it to the father. Conveniently, the only other survivors of Sodom are Lot's two daughters with whom he escapes to the city of Zoar. But Lot is afraid to stay there and flees once more *with his daughters*, this time to the rocky hill-country above the Dead Sea plain. They take refuge in a *me'arah* "cave," its sexual connotation obvious both psychoanalytically (Freud 1916-17:156) and linguistically with its associations to words such as *'arah* ("to be naked"), *'erwah* ("genitals"), *'arah* ("bare place"), *'eryah* ("nakedness"), *'arar* ("to strip oneself").[29]

The despairing daughters, who were betrothed in Sodom, conclude that not just Sodom but the whole earth has been laid waste, and that there are no men left. On two successive nights they give Lot wine (more fruit—but this time, fruit of the vine!), "lie with" him in a cave (the place where one "sleeps" with one's father), and "seduce" him into impregnating them. The narrative suggests that the father did not knowingly participate in this incestuous act. Lot was "unwittingly" seduced after being made drunk by his two daughters, just as Adam was "unwittingly" seduced by the woman he fathered. Although it is unclear just who he thought had stopped by the cave on the two sequential nights of his seduction, twice we are told that "he knew not when she lay down and got up." The man who offered his betrothed daughters to gang-rape deflowers them himself.

Patriarchal law decrees that the "product" of sexual union, the child, belongs exclusively to the father (Gallop 1989:109). In the case of Lot and his daughters, it would appear that this maxim is followed to the extreme. As virgins, Lot tells the Sodomites that they "had not 'known' a man" (Gen 19:8). These daughters "belong" exclusively to Lot. At the end of the narrative, the wombs that bear Lot's sons (Moab, lit. "from my father," and Ben-Ammi, lit. "son of my kinsman"!) are those of his two daughters, repossessed by Lot as a means of reproduction.

Lot's incestuous relationship with his daughters is not treated in the text as "wrong." Indeed, it goes unpunished and without further narrative comment.[30] But these stories are disturbing. Lot is "blamelessly" seduced by his daughters, just as Adam was "unwittingly" seduced by the woman he fathered. Daughters and fathers in Genesis . . . what is wrong with this picture?

5

OEDIPUS, SHMOEDIPUS, I LOVE MY MOM! THE BIBLICAL (DE-)CONSTRUCTION OF FEMALE SEXUALITY

> There is a well-known comic anecdote according to which an intelligent Jewish boy was asked who the mother of Moses was. He replied without hesitation: "The Princess." "No," he was told, "she only took him out of the water." "That's what *she* says," he replied.
>
> —Sigmund Freud (1916-17:161)

Psychoanalysis, we have known for a long time, is about human sexuality. It is also, as any reading of Freud confirms, about the possibilities and limits of narrative. One great virtue of the Hebrew Bible, which may explain its apparently endless capacity to generate commentaries, is that it too combines these elements.

In this chapter I juxtapose some of Freud's writings which deal with female sexuality and biblical narratives with the same theme.[1] I find that, as in (classic) Freudian theory, the biblical "mother" is a sexual female at the center of a battle between father and son, a catalyst initiating rivalry and hostility. In both Freud's texts and the Hebrew Bible, female sexuality can be seen as potentially menacing and therefore is "de-constructed."

It should be emphasized that my using a Freudian construct does not mean that I agree with all of Freud's views of women, nor that I consider Freud a biblical scholar. Instead, reading the

Hebrew Bible in conjunction with Freud brings an anterior text
out of a subsequent one. Freud is what comes to me, not as an
"authority" but as Iser's "foreshortened" text (see chapter 2,
above), which is, after all, a basic premise of this book.[2] Reading the Bible highlights the impossibility of reading outside the
"infinite" text, a text which for me includes both the Bible and
Freud.

SEXUALITY AS PROBLEMATIC

Biblical sexuality is problematic. Although in the Bible males do
"lie with" females in the context of "legitimate" sexual relations
(Uriah's reference to spending the night with his wife, 2 Sam
11:11, and the conception of Solomon, 2 Sam 12:24, are two
examples), the vast majority of the uses of the verb *shakab*
refers to rape (as in the rape of Dinah, Genesis 34), incest (e.g.,
Lot and his daughters, Gen 19:32, 34, 35), promiscuity (the
activities of Eli's sons, 1 Sam 2:22), seduction (the attempts of
Potiphar's wife to seduce Joseph, Gen 39:10, 12, 14), adultery
(the punishment of David that others will "lie with" his wives,
2 Sam 12:11), and forbidden relationships (such as an unclean
woman, father's wife and daughter-in-law, aunt, and homosexuality, Lev 20:11-19).[3]

Shakab also has numerous associations with death and
defeat. "To die" is to "lie" with one's ancestors (1 Kgs 1:21; 2
Kgs 14:22, etc.), and the dead are those who "lie" in the grave
(Ezek 32:21 and 29; Ps 88:6, etc.).

Certainly, associations of eroticism and destruction/death
have a long literary tradition. Emily Vermeule points to the
"ambiguity of slaughter and sex" and notes that Homer has "a
habit, at mocking moments, of treating enemies as lovers, fusing
the effects of Eros and Thanatos" (1979:157). Death itself has
been described as a lover (McClelland 1964:182-216) or as a
sexually potent goddess (Good 1982; Coogan 1978).

Attraction and revulsion, longing and fear, are co-existing
images of sexuality and death in biblical literature as well.
Commenting on Songs 8:6 ("Set me as a seal upon your heart,
as a seal upon your arm: for love is strong as death, passion is
hard as Sheol. Its flashes are flashes of fire, fiercer than any

flame"), Marvin Pope, for example, notes the association of love with death (1977:228-229); according to Francis Landy, because of the grammatical construction of the verse, Death "inevitably engage[s] Love" (1983:123); and Niditch emphasizes the metaphoric equation, reading this verse as an assertion that on some level "love is death and death love" (1989:43).

There seems to be a philological tradition tying eroticism to death as well. In many languages, the word translated as "to die" is used also to mean "have a sexual climax," especially for a man (e.g., Lat. *morticula*; Fr. *la petite morte*). As Louise Vasvari (1990) notes, it is possible that the associations are multiple: death-like spasms in the moment of orgasm and vice versa; men about to die often experience an erection; the male organ "dies" after climax; etc.

While the biblical concept of sexuality is problematic in general, female sexuality is particularly so. Simplistic as it may seem, female sexuality appears to be the chief source of male anxiety in the Hebrew Bible. Indeed, the sexually promiscuous female is the most common prophetic metaphor for a nation's disaster. In describing Israel, for example, Jeremiah states:

> You [female] are destroyed.[4] What will you do? Because you dressed in scarlet, because you decked yourself with golden ornaments, because you widened your eyes with paint, in vain you make yourself beautiful. Your lovers despise you, they will seek your life. (Jer 4:30)

And in Isaiah, Babylon, the virgin, will become the unhappy spoils of war, sexually humiliated and abused:

> Take millstones and grind flour; uncover your hair; expose your skirt; uncover your leg; pass over the rivers. Your nakedness will be uncovered and your shame will be seen. (Isa 47:2-3)

In Judg 5:27 images of vulnerability, petitions, and ignominious defeat in battle intertwine, bringing together the association of female sexuality with defeat and death. There Jael lures the enemy with gentle promises of comfort. Sisera, the warrior, "between her legs, destroyed—falls" in the sexual posture of a would-be lover, a vulnerable petitioner.[5] And this ambivalent role of woman as potential nurturer is not unique to Jael; the sexually active biblical woman invariably represents a fusing of Eros and Thanatos.

THE OEDIPAL CONFLICT

Why is biblical female sexuality so problematic? In (classic) Freudian theory, "mother" as a sexual female is at the center of a battle between father and son, a catalyst initiating rivalry and hostility; so too in the Hebrew Bible.

Biblical literature is often distinguished from other ancient texts by its apparent break with mythology's panoply of deities. Indeed, as Fishbane points out, "If one nostrum is widely accepted it is just this: . . . the Hebrew Bible reflects a primary rupture with the world of myth and mythmaking . . ." (1991:1).[6] Scholars have also noted, however, that many Hebrew Bible narratives strongly resemble the themes and language of ancient Near East mythic cycles. A prominent feature of these contemporaneous texts is the presence of strong goddesses and the fear they generate among male gods.[7]

Archaeological finds of god and goddess figurines seem to confirm that polytheism was prevalent in early Israel. As Bernhard Lang notes,

> During the four and a half centuries of Israelite monarchy (ca. 1020-586 BC), the dominant religion is polytheistic and undifferentiated from that of its neighbors. The religions of the Ammonites, Moabites, Edomites, Tyrians, etc., are local variants of the common Syro-Palestinian pattern which is not transcended by their individual traits and distinctive features. The original religion of Israel belongs to this group of West-Semitic cults. (1983:23)

Even more significant, female deities were at least as popular as male (Plaskow 1990; Teubal 1990). One explanation for this is that goddesses had a particular hold on women because of the numerous roles open to them in sacred rites. Women functioned as singers, dancers, diviners, dream interpreters, mourners, and priestesses (Ochshorn 1981: chap. 4; Harris 1976; Stone 1976: chaps. 7-8). A more obvious explanation, however, is that the concept of goddesses would have appealed directly to women's *maternal experiences*. Indeed, the numerous instances of railing against goddess-worship throughout the Hebrew Bible suggest that Ishtar continued to cast a long shadow, a shadow strikingly parallel to the "earliest love object" for all infants—the mother (Freud 1931b).

In Freudian theory, the primal bond to the mother foreshadows and overshadows later ties to the father. As Freud states, "We knew, of course, that there had been a preliminary stage of attachment to the mother, but we did not know that it could be so rich in content and so long-lasting . . ." (1916-17:583).[8] This primal bond is present also in Hebrew Scriptures. Ultimately, before the figure of the father-god stands the mother-goddess.

According to Freud's famous Oedipus theory (viewed, of course, from the perspective of the male child rather than that of the mother, father, or female child), the male child first loves his mother and his attachment to her becomes charged with phallic/sexual overtones. The boy views his father as a rival for his mother's love and wishes to replace him. Fearing retaliation (specifically, castration) by his father for these wishes, the male child experiences a conflict: love for his mother and fear of his father's power. The son's ego is transformed through the incorporation of paternal prohibitions to form his superego, and, eventually, he gives up his affinity for his mother, radically repressing and denying his feelings toward her while simultaneously identifying with his father. But these feelings are not fully repressed; they are expressed in sublimated activities, and the maternal shadow continues to be present. "The precursor of the mirror," writes Winnicott, "is the mother's face" (1971:117). Every step of the way, as the analysts describe it, a child "develops a relationship to father while looking back at mother" (Chodorow 1978:126). "Mother" becomes an internalized *imago* with two competing images. On the one hand, she is idealized, the womb being a protecting originator and sustainer of life. On the other hand, the boy links her sexuality with slaughter, since his desire for mother potentially castrates and kills (Freud 1916-17:488).

Freud's description of the family constellation and the role of the Oedipus conflict in sexual development (1925j) is strikingly parallel to the family constellation in the Hebrew Bible: God (as father), Israel as a construct of his (male) offspring, and the shadowy mother (the earlier, repudiated goddesses). Read within this framework, God-as-Father prohibits his male offspring from desiring the goddess/mother. Indeed, narrative after narrative describes YHWH chastising Israel for backsliding to earlier female deities.

Hearing the father's voice, what Freud calls the "superego" and what Lacan (in a play-on-words) calls *le non du père* ("the name/no of the father"), the son, as an embodiment of all the males of the community, identifies with the father image, that of the male deity. By doing so, Israel becomes a "kingdom of priests" (Exod 19:6). But, the pre-Oedipal, pre-patriarchal earliest love object, the mother, still lurks. This leads to a conflict.

On the one hand, biblical "motherhood" is construed as the ultimate destiny of essential womanhood. Narrative accounts amplify and clarify the importance of (male) offspring to a woman. "Give me children or I shall die," cries Rachel to Jacob (Gen 30:1), a plea repeated over and over throughout the biblical text. And although women appear in many roles in Hebrew Scriptures, it is a very rare woman who is not identified as the mother of a son, re-enforcing the position that the best thing that can happen to a young woman (the passive is significant here) is to have lots of (male) children. Throughout Genesis, indeed throughout the Hebrew Bible, the wombs of women "belong" to God. Eve, for example, the first to give birth, triumphantly declares, "I have gotten a man *with the help of the Lord*" (Gen 4:1); in Genesis 16, Sarah tells Abraham that YHWH has kept her from having children; Abraham, convinced of Sarah's sterility, is informed by God: "I will bless her, and moreover *I* will give you a son of her" (Gen 17:15). Rachel is so desirous of children that she uses a surrogate mother (Gen 30:3). The narrator then reports that "God remembered Rachel and *God* hearkened to her and *opened her womb*. And she conceived and bore a son" (Gen 30:21-24). The passage ends with Rachel's plea for more sons: "And she called his name Joseph, saying 'The *Lord add to me* another son.'" Freud thus sounds almost biblical when he writes that "a mother is only brought unlimited satisfaction by her relation to her son; this is altogether the most perfect, the most free from ambivalence of all human relationships" (1916-1917:597).[9]

On the other hand, the concept of "motherhood" is potentially menacing. Female procreative power (and its link to fertility goddesses) may be perceived as rivaling the sexual potency of the deity and/or the God-like male he created and by whom he is emulated. To countermand perceived female fecundity, God establishes the covenant of circumcision with the male members of this community, a contract which makes Abraham and his male offspring "exceedingly fruitful" (Gen 17:6), and thereby repudiates goddesses and their female devotees.[10]

CIRCUMCISION AND PATERNAL IDENTIFICATION

While biblical scholars have discussed the political and religious implications of this covenant, they have not paid much attention to the "token" which seals the arrangement.[11] Why the penis? Certainly, if the purpose was to distinguish Abraham and his household from all other people, a more obvious part of the body might have been chosen (e.g., piercing the ear or nose).

The sexual symbolism is powerful in its reverberations. The covenant is with Abraham alone. Sarah is not included. Instead, Sarah is mentioned only as the bearer of Abraham's "seed," which is blessed by God as though the patriarch's sperm were self-generating: "I will give to you *through her* a son" (Gen 17:16). Although both Abraham and Sarah are to be the fore-bearers of kings and nations, the covenantal relationship is with males exclusively, first with Abraham, and then with Abraham's son Isaac. Sarah is identified through the filter of Abraham's experience. Clearly, the covenant community is the community of males (Gen 17:10), and the essence of the arrangement is the multiplication of men. (And by head count alone, Abraham's grandson, Jacob, plays a very prodigious role in the "multiplication of men," since he sires twelve sons [and only one daughter]; by the time he goes to Egypt, moreover, he has accumulated sixty-six bloodline descendants—sixty-four of them male!)[12]

Since there is an implicit male erasure of the female role in procreation, the covenant of circumcision signifies that procreativity lodges in the relationship between God and human males. Male sexuality forms the nucleus of filiation (see Eilberg-Schwartz 1990), a common bonding, and the penis is the focus of the holy covenant.[13] The male organ is linked with power. Female sexuality is deconstructed. Sarah apparently supplies nothing of her essential being to the child and is merely the vehicle through which this covenantal relationship is established and maintained. Woman is the soil in which male "seed" is planted. "Semen as seed, the child in essence, the part for the whole . . . the child is fashioned solely by the impregnating principle provided by the father" (Mace 1953:248).[14]

Of course, this idea of conception is not unique to the Hebrew Bible. Aeschylus expresses the Greek view: "The mother is no parent of that which is called her child, but only the nurse of the new-planted seed that grows. The parent is he who mounts" (in Lattimore 1967).

CIRCUMCISION AND CASTRATION

Interestingly, however, this link with power, the penis, is to be circumcised. For Freud (1916-17:165; 1937c:122), circumcision is the "symbolic substitute" for castration, for what is no longer there. Since the circumcised penis both asserts the possible threat of castration (the foreskin has been removed) and denies it (the head of the penis is prominent as in an erection), from this perspective, the covenant between God, Abraham, and subsequent male offspring established in Genesis 17 reflects a chain of fathers and sons, and thereby the tensions of male power. Indeed, there are some interesting resonances in the terms of a relationship which stipulates that those who do not "cut" will be "cut off."[15]

> And the uncircumcised male who does not circumcise the flesh [lit. "meat"] of his foreskin, that person shall be cut off from the people; he has broken my covenant. (Gen 17:14)

Although YHWH promises to bless Abraham's "seed," he immediately establishes the vulnerability of Abraham's organ and

Abraham's dependence upon God for fertility. Certainly, no other part of the body would emphasize as effectively the connection between Abraham's reproductive capacity and the deity's ultimate potency, particularly since Abraham and the men of his household are circumcised as adults, an obviously memorable procedure.

Since the covenant endows the male with the ability to engender life, and then extends this ability from father to son, by implication Abraham now possesses God's procreative powers. The narrative account of the covenantal relationship is therefore a paradigm of the Freudian male-child's Oedipus conflict, the lure of which is affiliation with the father, the superiority of masculine identification and masculine prerogatives over feminine. As such, there is a potential threat to paternal authority and struggle is inevitable.[16] In fact, many scholars suggest that this motif is an important aspect of continuity between the books of the Hebrew Bible. David Jobling, for example, identifies antagonistic aspects of heredity in Judges and Samuel (1986:53), as does Alice Bach, who writes: "Beginning with the birth of Samuel, spiritual father to both Saul and David, and ending with the death of Saul and his sons, . . . coming of age . . . can be read as a record of war games of slaughter and betrayal" (1990a:37).

Circumcision can thus be seen as a partial castration, the price God-as-father exacts from Abraham-as-son (and his sons) to be in the analogous paternal position.

CIRCUMCISION AS FEMINIZING

There is another aspect to circumcision which highlights father-son relations. Circumcision symbolically feminizes. As the midrash asks:

> Why is it written, "And the Lord will pass over the door" [Exod 12:23]? . . . Read it [door] literally as "opening!" . . . the opening of the body. And what is the opening of the body? That is the circumcision (*Zohar*, 2:36a; in Wolfson 1987:204).

In Freudian analysis (as elsewhere), of course, the "door/gate" is a symbol of the female genital orifice (Freud 1916-17:156).

Thus, this sexual displacement, read from a psychoanalytic perspective, allows Israel to be portrayed as a female with respect to God, despite the fact that the covenant is made only with males.[17] Ezek 16:6 is a graphic example:

> I passed by you [feminine] and saw you [feminine] weltering in your blood, and I said to you [feminine] "Live in your blood."

Circumcision, therefore, has at least two ramifications in the Hebrew Bible. First, it enables the son to emulate the father. That is, in place of specific priests and priestesses of Ishtar dedicating their sexuality to the *goddesses* by engaging in ritual sexual intercourse in the *goddesses'* honor in order to celebrate and enhance the fertility of the *goddesses*, Abraham and his sons celebrate the fertility of a *male* deity and *male* procreativity. Implied within this construct, however, is a warning by the deity that "if you worship women I'll finish the job started by circumcision and *fully* castrate you to *make* you a woman."

This implied threat leads to the second ramification of circumcision: it symbolically insures that the son can never be as powerful as the father by metaphorically transforming male Israelites into females. That is, the circumcised men of Israel, the male "nation of priests" become "Daughters of Zion" (Boyarin 1992:475). In Lacanian terms, Abraham and his offspring may possess the penis, but never the Phallus, which is the ultimate symbol of paternal authority and the privilege it signifies. As a result, only the deity can provide a thoroughly intact "opener" of a womb.

As discussed in chapter 4 (above), although the word "Phallus" is interchangeable with "penis" in ordinary usage, this is not the case in that branch of psychoanalysis which concerns itself with psychosexual development. In the discourse of psychoanalysis, the word "Phallus" does not denote the anatomical organ "penis." Rather, it is the signifier or symbol of what we desire but lack—irrespective of which sex we happen to be—and it is most often associated with the concept of "power." Thus, in the words of Jacques Lacan, the Phallus is a sexually *neutral* "signifier of desire . . . the ultimate significative object, which appears when all the veils are lifted" (1958:252).

A biblical example of the significance of the "Phallus" and its potency is the account of the miracles in Exod 4:1-5 and 7:8-12, where Moses's and Aaron's "rods" become "snakes" and vice versa. A rod and a snake, to be sure, are time-honored phallic symbols in literature. Here they seem to represent both Freudian sexual symbolism (the two phases of the male organ in its active and quiescent states) and Lacanian phallic symbolism (the *power* of Moses and Aaron over Pharaoh). In the sequel, when Aaron performs the rod miracle, Pharaoh's sorcerers perform the same deed, but Aaron's rod (7:12) swallows up the sorcerers' rods, emphasizing "power" in the erect and hard condition. There is also an interesting subliminal sexual meaning—by metathesis *bala'* ("swallow") suggests *ba'al* ("possess") or *be'îlah* ("sexual intercourse").

THE "GENDER" OF GOD

It has been argued, of course, that the deity in the Hebrew Bible is not male and has no sex. Some feminist scholars, for example, enumerate female images of God such as mother (e.g., Num 11:12; Deut 32:11; Isa 46:3-4; 49:15-16; 66:13; Ps 131:2; Job 38:28-29) as well as wet-nurse and midwife (Trible 1978, chaps. 2 and 3), and formulate them as a counterbalance to a masculine characterization of YHWH. In addition, theological literature now stresses that the "Father" God and "Lord" God are not to be understood literally and naively. "God-names and properties have only symbolic significance" (Heine 1989:14). But what does "only" mean? It can be argued that feminist concerns for a female image of God seem a little forced, especially when the gender of a word is used as proof. To illustrate, the word "spirit" has a variety of genders depending upon the language: in German it is male, in Greek neuter, in Hebrew feminine, and in English, of course, nouns have no gender at all.

On the other hand, there is no doubt that male designations for the divine qualities and modes of action predominate in Hebrew Scriptures. Even attributes and actions that are themselves gender-neutral are read through the "filter of male language" (Plaskow 1990:123). There is nothing intrinsically male, for example, about the strangest of all God's names: "I shall be who I shall be" (Exod 3:14). Yet, when the issues are justice, law, anger, punishment, and power, God is portrayed using male terminology, male pronouns, and in terms of male characteristics and images. As Cynthia Ozick notes, the hand that leads Israel out of Egypt is a male hand, whether or not it is called so explicitly (1983:122). God is a man of war (Exod 15:3), a shepherd (most famously in Ps 23:1), a king (1 Sam 12:12; Ps 10:16), and a father (Deut 32:6; Isa 1:2-4; 64:7; Ps 68:6; 103:13; Prov 3:12). Most important, however, God bears the name "God *of* my Father" (Gen 31:5, 29, 42, etc.).

As many scholars have noted,[18] one of the most distinctive features of Genesis is the frequent use of a variation on the divine epithet "God of your/his/their *father*[s]," with "Abraham" and/or "Isaac" added in apposition to "father" (e.g., Gen 24:12; 28:13; 31:5, 29; 32:10; 46:1, 3). This appellation is particularly appropriate in the patriarchal narratives, since they revolve around the lives of fathers. Indeed, according to Peter Miscall, the text *is* the chronicle of the fathers: "That is the core, the essential meaning" (1983:4). Even when the epithet is not used, however, it is clear that Hebrew Scriptures describe the special, personal relationship of a particular male deity and a particular male community in terms of father and son.

SARAH

Despite this biblical resistance to female sexuality, for Genesis to chronicle the tribe's founding fathers, reproduction must occur. Since women are still the only source of sons, motherhood must be authorized for the sons of Israel to exist. Enter Sarah.

Gen 18:1-16 relates how Sarah, an old woman, overhears that she is to have a child, laughs spontaneously at what she perceives as a ridiculous idea, is embarrassed when confronted with her laughter, and denies having laughed. It reads:[19]

> YHWH appeared to him by the terebinths of Mamre as he was in the door of his tent in the heat of the day. He raised his eyes and looked and behold! three men stood by him. He saw, ran to call them from the door of his tent, and bowed to the ground. He said, "My Lord! please, if I have found favor

in your eyes, please do not pass from your servant. A little water, please, will be gotten. Wash your feet and rest under the tree. I will get a piece of bread. Sustain your hearts. After that you will go on since you have passed your servant." They said, "Yes. Do as you said." Abraham hurried to Sarah's tent and said, "Hurry! Three measures flour! Measure! Knead! Make cakes!" Abraham ran to the cattle, took a tender and good calf, gave it to the young man. He hurried to make it. He took butter, milk, and the calf which he prepared and set it before them. He stood before them under the tree and they ate. They said to him, "Where is Sarah, your wife?" He said, "Behold! In the tent!" "He said, 'I shall surely return to you at this season. Behold! A son lives for Sarah, your wife.'" Sarah heard at the door of the tent; he was behind it.[20] (Abraham and Sarah are old and coming in years. For Sarah, it had ceased to be after the manner of women.) Sarah laughed inwardly and said, "After I am shriveled! I shall have pleasure? My Lord is old!" YHWH said to Abraham, "Why is this that Sarah laughed saying, 'Is it indeed true that I shall bear a child? I am old!' Can't YHWH perform a wonder? At the appointed time I shall return to you at this season. A son lives for Sarah." Sarah denied, saying, "I did not laugh," (because she was afraid). He said, "No, but you laughed." The men got up from there and looked towards Sedom, and Abraham went with them to bring them on their way.

This apparently simple scene is complex and raises several questions. First, why is Sarah laughing? Biblical characters, as a rule, do not laugh. Indeed, throughout the entire Hebrew Bible, the verb "to laugh" is used only six times, and only in relation to Sarah's child-bearing.[21] In Gen 17:17 "Abraham fell upon his face and laughed" when he heard that Sarah was to have a child; Sarah then "laughed within herself" when she overheard the prophecy (Gen 18:12), an act which was questioned (18:13) and which she then denied (18:15), but with which she was confronted (18:15). After giving birth, Sarah predicts that once the news gets around, "All who hear will laugh" (Gen 21:6).

Second, why is Sarah condemned for laughing? After all, when Abraham heard the same news, prior to his circumcision, he found the idea so incredible and outrageous that he "fell on his face and laughed" (Gen 17:17).

Finally, who hears Sarah laughing? Because of the frequent use of indeterminate pronouns, and the seemingly inexplicable changes from singular to plural verb forms, this question has generated considerable commentary.

Traditional readings of Genesis 18 highlight Abraham's hospitality toward strangers and castigate Sarah for her "feeble attempt at deception" (Speiser 1964:131). But the several points of contact with the preceding narrative, which establishes the covenant between Abraham and God, allow another reading, one which highlights the biblical deconstruction of Sarah's sexuality. As the rabbis write: "Do not be misled by the chapter separation . . . It is all one story" (*Bereshit Rabbah* 48:4).

ABRAHAM'S VISION

Abraham, having just circumcised himself, has a post-surgical vision of the deity. That Abraham should be thinking about God at this time does not seem particularly surprising, since it was YHWH who had commanded the presumably painful medical procedure which had just taken place. In the midst of his musings, Abraham realizes that three visitors have arrived.[22] Not wanting his vision of God to disappear, Abraham calls out to the deity: "My Lord![23] please, if I have found favor in your eyes, please do not pass from your servant."

But Abraham has guests to entertain who are in need of food and rest. After eating, the guests question Abraham as to Sarah's whereabouts. Abraham, in a position to see his wife, responds: "Behold! In the tent!

It is with the next verse, the key which explains Sarah's laughter, that my reading of the narrative differs from traditional exegesis. Literally, Gen 18:10 reads, "He said, 'I shall surely return to you at this season. Behold! A son lives for Sarah, your wife.'" Most commentaries translate this verse as "Then one [of the men] said . . ." (see, e.g., Sarna 1989:130). But due to the indeterminate nature of the pronoun "he," I wish to propose an alternate reading: Abraham is not having *another* conversation, but rather *remembering* his earlier, dramatic dialogue with God, a discussion inspiring enough for the ninety-year old man to circumcise himself and his household. Abraham's thoughts *return* to his pre-surgical talk with YHWH and he muses over the promise. Abraham is reflecting audibly, loud enough for Sarah to hear: "He said, 'I shall surely return to you at this season. Behold! A son lives for Sarah, your wife.'" Read this way, Sarah hears Abraham's *re-enactment* of his conversation with God. That is, Sarah hears her aged husband, recuperating from a self-administered circumcision, speaking aloud—to himself—ruminating over the promise of a child.

The narrator interrupts the scene with an emphasized reminder that both Abraham and Sarah are extremely unlikely candidates for parenthood and underscores Sarah's advanced age by adding that she no longer menstruates. Not surprisingly, the post-menopausal Sarah, hearing her husband's words, "laughs within herself."

According to Freud, laughter is a response to a displaced version of a sexual or aggressive wish, and represents a fundamental rebellion against those social laws which regulate our sexual drives (Freud 1905c).[24] Even in Hebrew, the root *ts-ḥ-q* is used also in the context of "playing," with sexual connotations (e.g., Exod 32:6, or the more graphic Gen 26:8 and 39:17). But *why* does Sarah laugh? She speaks and reveals the reason: resentment of her aged husband who is unable to give her sexual satisfaction. "I shall have pleasure? My Lord is old!" The word she uses, *'ednah*, a cognate of Eden, resounds with images of lost sensual delight. The conclusion of some philologists that the word means "abundant moisture" makes it point even more directly to sexual physiology (Alter 1991:21; and Sarna 1989:130). "I shall have abundant moisture? My Lord is old!"

Abraham, hearing Sarah's words, realizes that his wife has overheard his audible recollection of YHWH's promise. Distressed, Abraham has another vision of the deity which includes another conversation. In this vision, however, there is a parapraxis, a "slip of the tongue" (Freud 1916-17:25).[25]

Although dreams provide our main access to the unconscious, there are also what Freud calls "parapraxes," unaccountable speaking errors, failures of memory, bunglings, misreadings, which can be traced to unconscious wishes and intentions. Freud instructed his followers to listen a little differently, since,

> . . . what results from the slip . . . has a sense of its own . . .
> the product of the slip . . . [is] a statement with a content and
> significance. . . . We must bear in mind . . . under what condi-
> tions, . . . why . . . the slip occurred in this particular way and
> no other, . . . and what it is that emerges in the slip
> itself. . . . (Freud 1916-17:32-35)

In this second vision of YHWH, Abraham represses Sarah's exact words, and alters them in two ways. First, Abraham falsely recalls Sarah asking if she shall indeed bear a child, a question Abraham wanted to hear but Sarah had not posed. Second and most important, Abraham suppresses Sarah's derision of his inability to give his wife sexual satisfaction, thus forming a defense against the reality of his own old-age. Sarah *is* beyond hope of pleasure—not because she is "shriveled" as Abraham would want to believe, but because of her aged husband and her sexual resentment toward him.

Abraham's sexual self-esteem, symbolically threatened by his circumcision, has been further endangered by Sarah's laughter. Sarah, realizing how upset her husband is, denies having laughed. Abraham confronts her: "No, but you laughed." Abraham's faulty reconstruction of the scene enables him to restore his self-esteem by diminishing Sarah's sexuality. Indeed, Abraham's version rings with Freud's misogynist views on the relative sexuality of aging males and females: "A man . . . strikes us as . . . youthful. . . . A woman of the same age['s] . . . libido has taken up final positions . . . it is as though the whole process had already run its course" (1916-17:598-599). Sarah's "motherhood" is affirmed, but her *jouissance* is denied.

THE "THREAT" OF FEMALE SEXUALITY

Abraham has made a covenant with YHWH which substitutes a "demythization" and denigration of female sexual experience for the Canaanite sacralization of female sexuality. The image of the breasts of the fertility-goddess nurturing the earth and the fields is replaced by the circumcised penis, a manifest symbol of the covenant contract between males.

But because this contract involves circumcision, with its attendant overtones of castration, male sexual vulnerability is displaced onto the female. As a result, all of the female characters throughout the Hebrew Bible (virgins, whores, mothers, concubines) share the hostility and possessiveness of men over their sexuality. The laws pertaining to women place them firmly under male control, first by fathers (or brothers), then husbands. Women's sexuality is even controlled by males beyond the grave: the law of levirate marriage (Deut 25:5-10) which requires Tamar to remain widowed regulates her sexuality for the sake of a dead husband and his line (Genesis 38).

There is yet other biblical legislation concerning female sexuality, such as laws about adultery (Num 5:11-31; Deut 22:23) and virginity (Deut 22:13-21). But these also speak to male advantage. For example, a man can bring his wife to trial even on suspicion of adultery (Num 5:11-31), but that right is not reciprocal. A girl whose lack of virginity shames her father on her wedding night can be stoned to death (Deut 22:13-21). An unbetrothed virgin who is raped *must* marry her assailant (Deut 22:28-29). Although the subject of these laws is women, the Bible does not address or even acknowledge the reactions of a raped girl married to her attacker, or the feelings of a wife accused of adultery by an unfaithful husband.

This anxiety about female sexuality is clearest in the complicated ritual and ideological systems of *tûmah* and *taharah*, terms usually translated as "uncleanliness" and "cleanliness," although more accurately described as "taboo" and "ritual purity." A woman with a normal menstrual period, for example, is "unclean" or "taboo" for seven days after the flow has ceased (Lev 12:2); after childbirth, for forty-one days in the case of a male child and eighty days in the case of a female child (Lev 12:2-6). While seminal emission also renders males "taboo," it is for one day only. Although it may be unfair to impose twentieth-century standards of "dirtiness" on the biblical construct of ritual purity, there is no doubt that these laws had the effect of preventing women from participating in sexual activities for a significant portion of their lives, regardless of their intent.

While Hebrew Scriptures describe various instances of harnessing women's sexuality, there seem to be few constraints in the text over male sexual needs. Indeed, female sexuality is depicted as negative in relation to positive or neutral male standards. The one exception is the Song of Songs, where positive female sexual imagery and potency abound, depicted as analogous to nature in general and the land in particular, the language of gardens, hillsides, plants, and animals predominating. Throughout the rest of the Hebrew Bible, however, male sexuality is accepted as a natural part of hu-*man* life and there is little denunciation of specific male sexual behavior, in contrast to female sexual prohibitions (Plaskow 1990:47).[26] Indeed, few transgressions are punished more severely than female sexual offenses. Promiscuity, a word repeated eighty-four times in the Hebrew Bible, is likened to "a woman out of control" (Setel 1985). Apparently, this means "out of the control of males," and therefore dangerous. Hos 2:4-5 is a typical example:

> Contend with your mother, contend; for she is not my wife, nor am I her husband. Let her therefore put away her harlotry out of her sight, and her adulteries from between her breasts, lest I strip her naked, and set her as in the day that she was born, and make her as a wilderness, and set her like a dry land, and slay her with thirst.

In this metaphor, not only is the promiscuous female to be physically punished, but there are broader implications as well. By using the promiscuous female as a metaphor for Israel, female sexual promiscuity is set in opposition to fertility.

CHILDLESS WIVES

Since biblical narratives portray motherhood as the only aspiration "deemed appropriate to [a woman's] 'real' sexual function within a patriarchy" (Rowe 1979:239), the sexuality of childless women is condemned throughout the Hebrew Scriptures.[27] Beginning with Eve, there is no clear license for female sexuality; indeed, the taboo the deity establishes immediately before creating her, an admonition given to Adam (the other male), implies a deconstruction of female sexuality before it is even constructed. When Eve is created, she is *not* authorized as Adam's sexual partner, but as his asexual "helper who is his counterpart." Although Woman may not have been created as a sexual being, having eaten of the "forbidden fruit," Eve sexualizes the garden and breaches the enclosure. As a result, throughout Genesis 1-3, Eve's role as Woman is under constant negotiation. Until her position in the family is fixed as the "'Mother' of All the Living" (which occurs only after the "Fall"), Eve is the crucial character. Yet her narrative centrality is in conflict with the repeated ways she is shifted from margin to margin. That is, until Eve has been evicted from the father's garden into motherhood, Eve—as a sexual female—is a problem. And the story of Eve is at the heart of the concept of Woman throughout the Hebrew Bible. She is Everywoman, the prototypical woman, all of her sex who are yet to come: "[the childless woman is viewed] as intrinsically evil; a foreign object, a sexual object, dirty. But in due course she becomes the mother of new members of the lineage. In the second capacity she is intrinsically good, the very criterion of virtue and cleanliness, the antithesis of a sexual object" (Leach 1983:74-75).

Even Sarah and Rebecca, before they become matriarchs, are endangered, because their husbands perceive their sexuality as a threat. In three places in Genesis a patriarch fears that his childless wife's beauty might become a source of danger to himself and claims that the woman is actually his sister (Gen 12:10-20; 20:1-18; 26:1-16). As I discuss in chapter 2, in each of these cases, the husband is willing to renounce his childless wife; the concession involves sex; and the patriarch becomes more powerful and wealthy as a result. Emotions clash uncomfortably and logic is twisted to prevent Abraham or Isaac from being condemned or condemning themselves. Indeed, the narrator does not blame the men for trading their wives in exchange for material gains, since a childless woman's beauty is a negative quality, perhaps one which causes the husband to have sexual self-doubts. Thus, it is "because of Sarai" who was "fair to look upon" that YHWH plagued Pharaoh and his house

(Gen 12:17), "because of Sarah" and "because of Rebecca" who were both "good to look at" that YHWH once closed (Gen 20:18) and once endangered (Gen 26:7) all of the wombs of the house of Abimelech.

Even the sexual desires of non-Israelite childless wives such as Potiphar's wife are condemned. Joseph is described as "good-looking *and* good to look at" (Gen 39:6). Even more importantly, her husband is a eunuch. At the very least, he is sterile and may possibly even be incapable of normal marital relations.[28] Yet the text shows neither sympathy for nor understanding of the Egyptian woman's sexual needs.

On the other hand, within the biblical text, a male's sexual needs are paramount, as indicated in the story of Genesis 38, (which immediately precedes this narrative). Judah, having been "comforted" after the death of his wife, seeks further "comfort" from a woman he presumes to be a prostitute but who is, in reality, his widowed, *childless* daughter-in-law Tamar. Within the biblical perspective, Judah's sexual needs can be fulfilled; however, Judah denies Tamar the opportunity to be equally "comforted" and commands her "remain a widow in your father's house" (Gen 38:11). By preventing Tamar from remarrying (by levirate marriage or otherwise) Judah condemns his daughter-in-law to silence.[29] Tamar, the widow, is precluded from participation in the economic and legal life of the community because she lacks identification with a family.[30] Equally egregious, Tamar is denied participation in a sexual relationship because Judah so decrees: after Judah discovers that he has impregnated Tamar, he "knew her again no more" (Gen 38:26).

DINAH

The story of Dinah, Jacob's only daughter, in Genesis 34, deals directly with male/female sexuality.[31] What makes this story particularly interesting is that, although it is reminiscent of the Abraham/Sarah, Isaac/Rebecca brother-sister-foreign male motif, Dinah is not a sister-wife, but an unmarried, *childless*, sister/daughter, and the question of sexual possession looms.

Dinah goes out alone one day from her father's house and is promptly seduced or raped by the local prince, Shechem.

Shechem, however, loves Dinah, and there is no indication that the attraction is not mutual. Shechem's desire for her is so great that he and his father go to Jacob, request Dinah as Shechem's wife, offer a covenant of mutual exchange of wives between the groups, and even agree that all the Shechemite men will have themselves circumcised in order to comply with Israelite laws. But Dinah's brothers, Simeon and Levi, are suddenly obsessed with a sense of outraged personal honor. This is something new to the Genesis text, particularly in light of Abraham's and Isaac's pandering in chapters 12 and 20. After deceptively agreeing to the pact, they wait until the third day after the circumcision, when the Shechemite men are incapacitated, at which time they pillage the town, kill all the males, and carry off all the wives and children. They seize Dinah from Shechem's house (does Dinah *want* to return home?) and depart. The act does not go entirely unpunished: Jacob is upset with the sons who broke the covenant and subsequently reduces their inheritance (Gen 49:5-7).

In this story, Dinah has no voice. But her silence is neither a natural nor an accidental phenomenon. The primacy of the male voice in this woman's story can be neither achieved nor maintained without an elaborate narrative strategy which includes the suppression of female sexuality. Indeed, throughout Genesis, narratively essential women are defined and described only in terms of their relationship to a male. In this narrative, for example, Dinah is called the *daughter* of Jacob (vs. 3), and the *sister* of Simeon and Levi (vs. 25). These family ties are maintained throughout the story: Jacob heard that Shechem had defiled *his daughter* (vs. 5); Shechem had done a disgraceful thing in defiling *Jacob's daughter* (vs. 7); Shechem talked to *her father* and *brothers* (vs. 11) who protested that they could not give their *sister* to one who is uncircumcised (vs. 14); if their conditions were not met, Simeon and Levi threatened to take their *daughter* and be gone (vs. 17);[32] Shechem had delight in *Jacob's daughter* (vs. 19); *her brothers* slaughtered all the Hivite males (vs. 25); and Simeon and Levi asked Jacob if Shechem should deal with their *sister* as with a whore (vs. 31). (It is somewhat ironic, moreover, that in the whole saga of the flood and the ark, in Genesis 6-9, Noah and his sons are continually named, but the identities of the four others saved with them—the grandmother and the three mothers of the whole human race to follow—are neither recorded nor considered in their own right!)

This biblical investment in only one sexuality, male, is highlighted in Simeon's and Levi's question (Gen 34:31): "Will he treat our sister like a whore?" Although the "he" is not specified, the brothers seem to be railing against Shechem: what must be protected, they argue, is "our view." That is, the female must conform to a male ideal, and that construct includes the reduction of any possible female complexity or sexuality.[33] Although the male may be castrated symbolically by circumcision, by de-constructing female sexuality, woman may be viewed as "really castrated." As a result, she becomes the guarantee against man's castration anxiety. That is, since females lack a penis, males have the Freudian and Lacanian sense of "presence." Viewed this way, Genesis 34 represents the subjugation of female desire to male rule by means of a continuum of violence, from the physical abduction of childless Dinah out of Shechem's house to the metaphysical violence exerted by the text.

MIRIAM

Although the focus of this book is Genesis, when discussing female sexuality, Moses' sister Miriam should be considered. Numbers 12 reports that Miriam spoke against Moses. As a result, she was stricken with a somewhat mysterious affliction. Childless, her disease (tsora'at) is the same as the venereal discharge described in Lev 22:4.[34] Her "offense" extends beyond discussing her brother Moses' sexual behavior; indeed, it is replete with its own sexual allusions.

Although there is a reluctance among some biblical scholars to read the book of Numbers in its final form, Fewell's and Gunn's argument for reading Judges 4 and 5 sequentially are just as valid here: ". . . why not do the obvious thing and try reading . . . as a single story" (1991a:390). If we do, Miriam's punishment follows the account of those who left Egypt having "lusted a lust," leading one to search for a deeper dynamic in the desert than a churning stomach. Certainly, that for which they "lusted"—meat—has a double meaning today, and the word apparently has the same sexual innuendo for Ezekiel who chastises Israel with this sexual imagery: "You have harloted with the sons of Egypt, your neighbors of large *meat*" (16:26). Equally graphic is Ezek 23:20: "She lusted after her lovers whose *meat* was like those of asses and seed like that of horses."

YHWH certainly seems to view Miriam's offense as having a sexual origin. He compares Miriam to the young woman who is publicly humiliated by her father and has to "bear her shame for seven days," an expression used often in the context of humiliation—for a *sexual* offense (e.g., Jer 22:22).

Moses also considers his sister's illness venereal. His warning to the Israelites that they must follow certain procedures in dealing with this disease begins with a reminder that Miriam was similarly afflicted and follows three legal sections, each having *sexual* ramifications for women.

First, a man who divorces a woman may not remarry her after the death or divorce of her second husband, because *she is now sexually defiled* (Deut 24:4).

Second, a "handmill" must not be taken in pawn, for that would be taking someone's life in pawn (Deut 24:6). Since this word (*rēḥayim*) is also the dual form of *reḥem* ("uterus"), the word "handmill"—a pair of stones with holes in their centers—-can be understood as a metaphorical off-color colloquialism referring to a female with a *sexual* function, perhaps a concubine or a child-bearing slave, thus making "woman" and "vulva" synonymous. This reading seems to be reinforced by Job who uses "grinding" as a sexual metaphor in 31:10 (and in rabbinic literature, the rabbis quip that a man's wife is a "millstone around his neck" [*Kiddushin* 29b]).

Third, if a man kidnaps and "abuses" a fellow Israelite, he must receive the death penalty (Deut 24:7). The reflexive tense of this verb (*hit'ammer*) can involve *sexual* possession and domination, as is clear from an analogous usage in the case of a captured foreign woman (Deut 21:14). From the male perspective, childless Miriam's sexuality results in *tsora'at*.[35]

PHALLOCENTRISM AND LOGOCENTRISM[36]

Throughout this chapter I have juxtaposed, rather than hierarchically positioned, Freud's views about female sexuality with those reflected in the Hebrew Bible. Reading Genesis and Freud simultaneously, it seems difficult to distinguish their respective ideas: "We might lay it down," writes Freud, "that . . . sexuality . . . is of a wholly masculine character" (1905d:217-218). In biblical narratives, as in Freud, female sexuality is explicitly subordinated to and subsumed by the male.[37]

Not surprisingly, Freud's constructs of female sexuality have resulted in varying intensities of dissent. Even analysts as early as Jones write that "men analysts have been led to adopt an unduly phallo-centric view" of female psychosexual development (1927:459).

More recent feminist critiques of Freud's "Female Sexuality" (1931b) and the Dora case (1905e) engage the issue of Freud's preconceptions of femininity.[38] As Christine Froula points out, Freud makes subtle war on woman's desire-language in order to avert its perceived threat to the father's cultural preeminence (1989:121). This statement could also be applied to the Hebrew Bible. Similarly, Juliet Mitchell points out that psychoanalysis can hardly avoid being phallocentric in a society organized along patriarchal lines: "If psychoanalysis is phallocentric, it is because the human social order that it perceives refracted through the individual human subject is patrocentric" (1975:xv). This criticism also sounds like that voiced by many biblical scholars.

As Simone de Beauvoir argues, men have established an absolute human type, the male, against which women are measured. Men are always the definers, women the defined (1961:xv-xvii). Certainly, Freud defines female sexuality in terms of the male: "She has seen *it* and knows that she is without *it* and wants to have *it*. . . . As regards little girls, we can say of them that they feel greatly at a disadvantage owing to their lack of a big, visible penis, that they envy boys for possessing one and that, in the main for this reason, they develop a wish to be a man—a wish that re-emerges later on, in any neurosis that may arise if they meet with a mishap in playing a feminine part" (Freud 1925j:252; 1916-17:318; emphasis added).

Likewise, the Hebrew Bible makes phallocentrism synonymous with logocentrism. Throughout the Scriptures, it is primarily the male characters who have defined "woman" and "man," and in the two-thousand some years of biblical interpretation, it is male-dominated discourse which has "cast in stone" these constructs. The covenant of Genesis 17, symbolized by the circumcised penis, has resulted in the "erection" of a paternal logos through the denial, or misnaming, of female sexual experience. Reconstructing biblical female sexuality reveals the textual struggle of women within and against this patriarchy.

6

AFTERWARDS

All of this having been written, so what? Since there can be no doubt that my readings of these biblical narratives are idiosyncratic, why read my readings?

First, I hope that I have conveyed the idea that biblical narratives cannot be discussed in any absolute sense. Certainly, my reading is no closer to the "true meaning" than any other interpretation. As I argue throughout, I view interpretation to be a *reader's* response, necessarily based on a *reader's* personal input, assumptions, and biases. For example, I take my own feminist stance as an explicit starting point. As such, I attend to the issue of gender and accord a privileged status to the experience and interests of the female biblical characters. I am aware, however, that this particular bias has implications with which biblical scholars who follow a different approach might disagree. As Freud stated in the preface to the Hebrew translation of his *Introductory Lectures on Psychoanalysis*, "Much [of this text] contradicts traditional opinions and wounds deeply-rooted feelings . . . it is bound . . . to provoke" (1916-17:11). But if I have been successful in my endeavor, then all our readings can co-exist.

Second, I approach the Hebrew Bible as a single literary work, unlike many biblical scholars who see it in terms of discrete "strands" which they identify as "sources," "traditions," or "literary forms." While it is tempting to resolve textual ambiguities by resorting to the common assumption that narrative "problems" are a result of the conflation of these sources, my concern is their *literary* effect. Although questions of constituent sources, redactional alterations, and so forth are important (particularly for scholars interested in historical source material, the history of a text, or the background of theological ideas), what I (along with many others) have tried to show is that it is not the *only* way of reading the Hebrew Bible. For this reading, traditional questions of sources do not apply.

Third, my theoretical approach is literary, not psychoanalytic, although it is clearly informed by psychoanalytic theory. Unfortunately, the relationship between "literature and psychoanalysis" usually implies a relationship of subordination rather than coordination. Literature is submitted to the "authority," to the "prestige," of psychoanalysis (Felman 1980:5). The literary text is considered as a body of language to *be* interpreted, while psychoanalysis is a body of knowledge used *to* interpret. What I have tried to do throughout this book is to read Freud and the Bible concurrently rather than to provide a hierarchical positioning. That is, I have not been reading the Bible *in light* of Freud, but rather *while reading* Freud. Therefore, I hope that I have shown that it is possible to juxtapose Freud and the biblical text without agreeing with all of Freud's views, particularly his views of women. Certainly, I do not consider Freud a biblical scholar. Rather, I appropriate Freud's psychoanalytic *approach* as another tool for biblical interpretation.

Finally, as many others have stated, it is not *easy* to read the Bible without the burden of other interpretations and commentaries obscuring our vision. What I have tried to do throughout this book, however, is to show that we *also* invest Scriptures with our own characteristic clusters of wishes—our fantasies—and transform these fantasies into the kind of significance we find meaningful: intellectual, social, moral, and/or aesthetic. In other words, my relation to Adam and Eve, Abraham and Sarah, Lot and his daughters, Dinah, Miriam, Moses, and the entire litany of biblical characters (including, in particular, the deity) has something to do with the murky complexities of my everyday relations with the people around me. As a reader, I do not simply identify with a character, and then live through the plot with him or her; my *form* of identification and, consequently, my view of the characters changes as the plot develops. Abraham and Sarah are human and make mistakes—perhaps that is enough for *me* to have learned.

111

NOTES

BIBLIOGRAPHY

INDEXES

NOTES

NOTE TO THE EPIGRAM

[1] One day, Auntie Ilona was telling her nephew Tyler, age two and a half, the story of the tower of Babel. "Once upon a time," she said, "everyone spoke the same language. Everybody understood what every single word meant. Because all the people on earth could talk to each other, they felt very smart. The people felt so clever, in fact, that they thought they could build a tower whose top could reach all the way to heaven and then they would be just like God! God came down to see this tower and wasn't too happy. Although God was proud of his children for working together and helping each other, God didn't like the idea that they thought they were so smart. God decided that this tower should not be built. The way to stop them was to confuse their words. So, God gave the people all different languages. From that time on, words *didn't* mean the same thing to everybody. And now, when people hear words in a different language, it sounds as though they are saying 'Ishkabibble-fribble.'"

Later that afternoon, Tyler's Great-Grandma came to visit. Great-Grandma had been born in Hungary and spoke only Hungarian. Tyler had been born in Atlanta and spoke only English. Great-Grandma loved Tyler very much and although she knew that he probably couldn't understand her, she told him just how much she loved him—in Hungarian. Tyler listened very carefully, kissed Great-Grandma and said, "Ishkabibble-fribble!"

NOTES TO CHAPTER 1:
READING (ABOUT) THIS READING

[1] For a general overview of the relationship of literature and psychoanalysis see Kurzweil and Phillips (1983); Skura (1981); Felman (1980); and Hartman (1978).

[2] On the other hand, this approach can be very illuminating for the way it highlights figures of repetition and the writer's use of "typical symbols."

[3] Among the better known articles is that of Jones (1948) who, taking as his basis Freud's observation that Hamlet's indecision was

rooted in his Oedipal entanglements with his father and mother, attributes Hamlet's indecisive behavior to suppressed feelings of hate and love followed by paralyzing guilt.

[4] The issue of characterization in biblical poetics has received considerable attention recently. See, for example, Gunn and Fewell (1993); Sternberg (1985); and Berlin (1983).

[5] McKnight's quotation cited above sounds almost like a paraphrase of this early "reader-response" critic!

[6] The concept of the reader has been subjected to a searching analysis and is a matter of considerable controversy among literary theorists. "Is he the 'Actual Reader' (Van Dijk, Jauss), the 'Super-reader' (Riffaterre), the 'Informed Reader' (Fish), the 'Ideal Reader' (Culler), the 'Model Reader' (Eco), the 'Implied Reader' (Booth, Iser, Chatman, Perry), or the 'Encoded Reader' (Brooke-Rose)?" (Rimmon-Kenan 1983:118). Wright has recently identified yet another species, what might be called the "Personally Desiring and Aspiring Reader" (1984:61), although Wright claims that in the process of analyzing the response of a reader, the second element (i.e., "aspiring") takes over.

[7] In Freud's discussion of the formation of character, he describes the character-traits of orderliness and obstinacy, found together with fair regularity, as "anal," and uses Alexander the Great as an example: "A striking allusion to this connection is to be seen in the legend that Alexander the Great was born during the same night in which a certain Herostratus set fire to the celebrated temple of Artemis at Ephesus out of a sheer desire for fame. So the ancients would seem not to have been unaware of the connection" (Freud 1916-17:566).

[8] See, e.g., Alter (1991) and Bar-Efrat (1989).

NOTES TO CHAPTER 2:
INTERTEXTUALITY AND TRANSFERENCE

[1] Freud first broaches the idea of transference in his technical contribution to the Freud and Breuer *Studies on Hysteria* (1895d). He returns to it in his "Dora" analysis (1905e). But his main discussions of the subject are found in his papers on technique: in particular, "The Dynamics of Transference-Love" (1912b), which deals with the theoretical side of the phenomenon, "Observations on Transference-Love" (1915a), which is concerned with the technical difficulties raised by positive transference, and the chapter "Transference" in his *Introductory Lectures on Psychoanalysis* (1916-17:431-447). Freud approaches the subject once more in "Analysis Terminable and Interminable" (1937c:216-253).

[2] One example is the Babylonian epic of Creation, where a number of themes occur twice in similar form. For instance, the story of the birth of Ea and the description of his personality are the same as those of Marduk; the preparations of Apsu and Mummu to destroy the gods parallel those of Tiamat and her allies; Ea's combat against Apsu and that of Marduk against Tiamat coincide. There are also identical passages reiterated three or four times: the portrayal of the monsters formed by Tiamat to help her in her struggle occurs four times. Similar instances are to be found in Ugaritic literature, which is nearest to the ancient Hebrew writings.

[3] See Fewell (1992) which is, to my knowledge, the first book to address literary intertextuality as it relates specifically to interpretation of the Hebrew Bible.

[4] Rabbinic exegesis offers a model, as suggested by the term *midrash* itself, taken from the root *d-r-sh*, "to study, to seek." This relation of rabbinic commentary to contemporary critical thinking has received much attention. See, e.g., Hartman and Budick (1986) and Handelman (1982).

[5] See, e.g., Kugel's polemical reproach that literary methods ignore the Bible's religious character (1981:217-236); see also the reply by Berlin (1982:323-327) and Kugel's response (1982:328-332).

[6] Polzin's seminal article (1975) discusses the primary relationship(s) of males and females as reflected in the patriarch/wife/foreign king stories in Genesis. Miscall (1979) argues for an extension of Polzin's study to include the Abigail/David and David/Bathsheba stories (1 Samuel 25 and 2 Samuel 11-12) on the basis of a more general view of the characters involved, and develops a series of five narratives which take the form of a moral treatise. In the cases cited by Miscall, however, sex is not necessarily uninvited by the woman, or at least not overtly resisted.

[7] See Jeansonne's discussion of Hagar as a powerless woman (1990:43-52).

[8] See Trible (1984:9-35) for a particularly lucid yet disturbing reading of Judges 19-21.

[9] Ricoeur (1970:573) calls this aspect of discourse analysis the wish for "recognition." Hartman (1975:37) refers to it as the wish for "presence," or for a "relationship."

[10] Deut 22:22, e.g., states that "if a man is found lying with a woman who is a *be'ulat-ba'al* they will die, the two of them." Similarly, Isa 54:1 states that "more are the sons of the desolate than of the *be'ûlah*." Here "sons-of-the-desolate," the chiasmas to the *be'ûlah* is negative since the verb *sh-m-m* is often applied to land which is

plundered, raped, and destroyed (see, e.g., Isa 49:8; Ezek 33:28). When used in the adjectival form in relation to people, sh-m-m connotes being destroyed by the enemy (in the "rape of Tamar" episode of 2 Samuel 13, Tamar remains shômēmah in the house of her brother Absalom). Isa 62:4 also sets the be'ûlah in opposition to the "desolate."

[11] What is even more fantastic, of course, is what happens subsequently. However, Sarah's "surpassing beauty" is a theme which fascinated Jews of antiquity, receiving attention in many sources (see, e.g., Gen 12:14-15; 26:7; Gen. Apoc. 20.1-9; Ant. 1.8.1; Gen. R. 40.4; Meg. 14a; BB 58a; Sanh. 39b).

[12] See, e.g., harog used to describe Cain's slaying of Abel (Gen 4:8), Esau's plan to murder his brother (Gen 27:41), and the mass slaying of the men of Shechem by Simeon and Levi (Gen 34:25-26).

[13] Niditch, e.g., contends that "the language of the account suggests that Abram relates to Sarai lovingly and implies that they undertake the trick together" (1987:57, emphasis added).

[14] See also Gen 24:51, where Laban expresses similar exasperation when he tells the servant that Rebekah may go after his attempts to keep her have failed.

[15] Miscall (1983:42) comments on Abraham's wealth and concludes that it was acquired improperly since it is not accompanied by the birth of a child and is therefore not a sign of blessing.

[16] One of the first scholars to make this observation is Miscall (1983:32). See, in particular, the discussions by Fokkelman (1987:48) and Clines (1990:75-77).

[17] See de Man (1979) for a general discussion of the issue of causation as motive and intentions.

[18] It has often been noted that the remark presupposes a matrilineal system, for a man marrying the daughter of his father would avoid incest only on the assumption that the blood-line passes through the mother (see, e.g., Good 1981:95).

[19] Niditch (1987:55), on the other hand, argues differently. She claims that Abraham explains that Sarah is his half-sister "at a point of genuine heart-baring."

NOTES TO CHAPTER 3:
WHOSE DREAM IS THIS, ANYWAY?

[1] Freud discusses this model of dream theory principally in Chapter VII of *The Interpretation of Dreams* (1900a), and in the

chapters on dreams in the *Introductory Lectures on Psychoanalysis* (1916-17).

2 See Arlow and Brenner (1964) for a general description of, and distinction between, these two theories of dream analysis.

3 See, e.g., Oppenheim (1956) and Niditch (1980).

4 Two of the most fascinating readings of the Joseph narrative are Schwartz (1990a) and Frieden (1990).

5 See chapter two (above) for a discussion of *be'ulat ba'al*.

6 See Gesenius' discussion on the use of the *futurum instans* (1909:360); see also Andersen (1974:94) and Berlin (1983:62) for rhetorical uses of this grammatical construct.

7 In chapters 2 and 3 of *Beyond the Pleasure Principle* (1920g) Freud raises two serious difficulties with the wish-fulfillment theory of dreams. First, people who have experienced a shock regularly dream about the trauma, and second, there are dreams which bring to conscious memory the earliest years of childhood which are linked to painful impressions of anxiety, prohibition, disappointment, and punishment. In both of these cases, Freud questions the wishful impulse which could be satisfied by going back to distressing experiences. He attempts to resolve the issue by claiming that there must be *some* wish-fulfillment of which neither the analyst nor the patient is aware, but which can be discovered over time.

8 See note 7.

9 As I discuss in chapter 2 (above), there seems to be little doubt that sexual intercourse with Pharaoh occurred, since Pharaoh states directly "I took her to me as a wife" (Gen 20:19), the same phrase used in reference to Hagar and Abraham which resulted in the birth of Ishmael.

10 There is, however, a certain tension between the dreamer and the reader, between a hermeneutics of correspondence and a method of association or displacement (see Frieden 1990). A dreamer interpreting his or her own dream searches for similar dream thoughts that lie behind dream contents in a condensed yet corresponding form. Drawing from the associative approach, a reader, like a psychoanalyst, uses connections provided by the dreamer which relate to the dream contents by contiguity, not by resemblance. These two interpretive models stand opposed, yet they also tend to blur into each other. The opposition has heuristic value here, as does the related distinction between metaphor and metonymy. See, e.g., Jakobson and Halle (1975:72-76, 90-96); for a discussion of the unstable interactions between metaphor and metonymy, see de Man (1979:12-15).

According to Freud, one of the primary aspects of dream work entails displacement, a relationship by *contiguity*. Freud writes that "the individual dream thoughts are represented in the dream by multiple elements" (1900a:318). Moreover, "the elements in the dream content which stand out as the essential components by no means play the same role in the dream thoughts" (1900a:340). Disparities are even more compelling when the dream contents have been displaced and have received a completely new center of interest.

[11] See, e.g., Frieden (1990).

[12] On the prophet as intercessor, cf. Exod 32:11, 34:8f, and Num 14:13-19 (Moses); 1 Sam 7:8; 12:19, 23 (Samuel); Amos 7:2; Jer 7:16; 37:3; 42:2. See also Rodes (1977:107-128).

[13] The Hebrew imperative frequently expresses a consequence expected with certainty, or an intention. As Gesenius describes, this is particularly the case when depending upon a jussive (a *wāw copulative* cohortative) (1909:325).

[14] This is Weber's descriptive term which calls attention not only to the scenic, theatrical aspects of the dream, but to its narrative moment as well (1982:171, n. 1).

[15] The narrator emphasizes the technical, judicial formula used in connection with the royal transfer of property, "took . . . gave" (Labushagne 1974:176-80).

[16] Rabbinic commentary (Gen. R. 52.12) is quite divided on this verse. Shadal reads it literally; Rashbam and Bekhor Shor figuratively. See also Weinfield (1985) for a contemporaneous legal interpretation.

[17] Holland has appropriated Freud's interpretive models of fantasy-and-defense to describe a similar transaction between an author's characteristic psychic style and a reader's, a distillation of what he calls an "identity theme."

NOTES TO CHAPTER 4: DAUGHTERS AND FATHERS IN GENESIS

[1] For the use of concubines and handmaidens in this early period and the legitimacy of offspring from such unions, see Archer (1987:4).

[2] Not all scholars view intercourse between siblings as incestuous. Fokkelman, e.g., takes this position in discussing the story of Amnon and Tamar (1981:103). As Landy points out, however, this might be another example of a royal family that "feels itself too good for the world" (1983:307, n. 63).

[3] Certainly Jacob views Reuben's act as a violation of family purity laws. In Gen 49:4, Jacob censures Reuben for "going up to" his

father's bed and "defiling" it. The verb Jacob uses, *hillalta*, is from the stem *ḥ-l-l* ("pollute, defile, profane") and is used in connection with sexual depravity (see, e.g., Lev 19:29; 21:9).

[4] According to Freud, shame is "considered to be a feminine characteristic *par excellence* . . . [and] has as its purpose, we believe, concealment of genital deficiency" (1916-17:596).

[5] Indeed, all of the following biblical Hebrew words can be translated as "shame," and the differences in meaning are slight, if existent at all: the verbs ("to shame") *b-w-sh*, *k-l-m*, *q-l-h*, *h-p-r*, *sh-p-l*, *m-k-k*, *ḥ-r-p*, *q-l-s*, *l-'-g*, and *l-y-ts*; and the nouns ("shame") *bûshah*, *bashnah*, *boshet*, *kelimmah*, *kelimmût*, *qîqalôn*, *shiplah*, *nablût*, *nebalah*, *ḥerpah*, *qeles*, *la'ag*, and *latsôn*.

[6] Indeed, as Danna Nolan Fewell has reminded me, a significant portion of the vocabulary associated with "guilt" is strictly cultic in usage, for example, as in "guilt offerings." The Hebrew verbs *'asham*, *rasha'*, and *'awon* can be translated as "to be guilty"; the nouns *'asham*, and *'ashmah* as "guilt"; and the adjectives *'ashēm* and *rasha'* as "guilty." See Bechtel (1991:54) for a detailed discussion of "shame" and "guilt" in the Hebrew Bible.

[7] Other anthropological models do exist, however. Among the Nuer, e.g., "fatherhood" belongs to the person in whose name cattle bridewealth is given for the mother (Rubin 1975:169).

[8] Paternal half-sister prohibition was of special concern to Ezekiel (22:11), and his concern shows that the practice continued.

[9] We might note that Moses and Aaron were both born of such a union (Exod 6:20; Num 26:59).

[10] The other incestuous relations itemized in Leviticus 18 and 20 belong to the category of incestuous adultery (i.e., group-wife prohibitions) or pertain to polygamy and therefore are not our concern here. For a full analysis of the incest laws in Leviticus, their function and origin, see Bigger (1979) and Fox (1967). For a situating of these laws in the wider context of historical shifts in Jewish social structure and the changing position of women, see Archer (1990 and 1983).

[11] Contra Wegner (1992).

[12] See Douglas's chapter on "Internal Lines" (1966) for an examination of the connections between social pollution and cultural ideas of "dirt."

[13] The editors of the *Standard Edition* trace (without critique) the vicissitudes of Freud's acknowledgement of sexual abuse on the part of fathers in a note to "Femininity" (Freud 1916-17:584-585).

[14] See, e.g., Miller (1984), as well as Herman and Hirschman (1981) who present clinical evidence; Balmary (1979) for a psycho-

analytic reading of the "text" of Freud's life and work; and Rush (1980) for an historical perspective. See particularly Willbern's examination (1989) of the chronological complexities and fluctuations in Freud's theorizing about fathers and daughters, including a discussion of Freud's discounting of the seduction theory and his strangely unprofessional alteration of several case testimonies in which the father had been identified as the incestuous seducer of his daughter.

[15] See, e.g., Laplanche and Pontalis (1968:17), for whom the daughter's seduction story is a fantasy, its reality "to be sought in an ever more remote and hypothetical past (of the individual or the species) which is postulated on the horizon of the imaginary and implied in the very structure of the fantasy."

[16] According to Freud, the mother becomes the original seducer, the original erotic manipulator of the infant, both male and female. "The fact that the mother thus unavoidably initiates the child into the phallic phase is, I think, the reason why, in phantasies of later years, the father so regularly appears as the sexual seducer" (1931b:238).

[17] See, e.g., Trible (1983) who points out that in Chapter 1 the masculine exists no more than does the feminine.

[18] In Gen 1:26, God says that he will make Adam ("humankind") in his image and "they will rule" (*wayirdû*) over the earth. It is then reported in 1:27: "male and female he created them." Since "Adam" is a generic term for "humankind" which has two sub-types, male and female, it can be read that Adam and Eve were created simultaneously and equally as two separate beings in Genesis 1:26.

[19] For a fascinating reading of the way the denied maternal occupies various interstices of the garden story, see Froula (1983).

[20] Girard's theory of language and culture explains the marginal situation of biblical daughters in a way that challenges Freud's theory of the Oedipus complex. Girard (1986) argues that violence has its roots in "mimetic desire," an approach/avoidance concept which describes the drive to imitate a respected and feared model. While the desire is to imitate, there is the recognition that a complete reproduction would result in an implicit rivalry, the extreme form of which would be displacement and ultimately, elimination. On the other hand, if this rivalry is rejected and repressed, the subject is then in a slave relationship with the master.

[21] According to Ragland-Sullivan, "The phallic signifier does not denote any sexual gender" (1986:271). Similarly, Rose attributes a sexual neutrality to the phallus by characterizing it as "a term which, having no value itself . . . can represent that to which value accrues" (1982:43). Jameson maintains most strenuously the difference between

the Lacanian phallus and the sexual organ. "This is the place to observe that the feminist attacks on Lacan, and on the Lacanian doctrine of the Signifier, which seem largely inspired by A. G. Wilden, 'The Critique of Phallocentrism,' . . . tend to be vitiated by their confusion of the penis as an organ of the body with the phallus as a signifier" (1977:352).

22 It could be argued that the text also represses father-son homosexuality.

23 As Frye (1982:107) writes, "The chief point made about the creation of Eve is that henceforth man is to leave his parents and become united with his wife. That parent is the primary image . . . that . . . has to give way to the image of the sexual union of bride-groom and bride."

24 A *mishteh* ("feast," "banquet") is usually an occasion for drinking. See, e.g., 1 Sam 25:36; Isa 5:12; Esth 2:18; 5:14; 8:17; 9:19.

25 See Malina (1985) for an excellent discussion of hospitality.

26 Finding additional support with the story of the rape of the Levite's concubine (Judg 19:22-30), Lerner (1986:175) concludes that these two narratives shows that "the virgin daughters are as disposable as the concubine or the enslaved women captured in warfare." Of course, many scholars argue for the dependence of Judges 19 upon Genesis 19. See, e.g., Soggin (1981:282, 288); Culley (1976:56-59); Moore (1976:417-419); and Burney (1970:443-444). See also Gunn (1974:294, especially note 1). But cf. Niditch (1982:375-378), who argues for the primacy of Judges 19 over Genesis 19. However, another approach views such stories as type-scenes without specific literary dependence; cf. Alter (1981:47-62). For recent discussions of these stories, see Fewell and Gunn (1993, chapter 5); Alter (1990); Trible (1984:65-92); Horner (1978:47-58); and Boswell (1980:92-98).

27 See chapter 2, above, for a discussion of Abraham, another "male protector," as procurer.

28 According to both Lerner and Sarna, the additional comment provided in verse 16 (*behemlat YHWH*, "the Lord being merciful to him") anticipates verse 29 ("God remembered Abraham and sent Lot out of the midst of the overthrow, when he overthrew the cities in which Lot dwelt" and indicates that Lot is not being saved for his own virtue but because of God's mercy and because of Abraham (Lerner 1986:172; Sarna 1966:150).

29 See Gunn (1980) for a fascinating discussion of this sexual metaphor in 1 Samuel.

30 Vawter (1977:242) argues that "this story, tenuously connected with the preceding narrative, obviously had little to do with the

Sodom and Gomorrah saga and owes it preservation to other concerns."

NOTES TO CHAPTER 5:
OEDIPUS, SHMOEDIPUS, I LOVE MY MOM!

[1] Freud's principal works on the sexual life of human beings are his *Three Essays on the Theory of Sexuality* (1905d:135-243) and "Some Psychical Consequences of the Anatomical Distinction between the Sexes" (1925j). For recent representative neo-Freudian reviews and critiques of Freud's ideas, see Mitchell (1975:1-131) and Irigaray (1977:34-67).

[2] "Whatever we have read sinks into our memory and is foreshortened. It may later be evoked again and set against a different background with the result that the reader is enabled to develop hitherto unforeseeable connections" (Iser 1974:125).

[3] In some instances in the Masoretic text, the object of *shakab* has been vocalized to suggest a direct object of a transitive verb, as in the English slang "to lay her" (see, e.g., Lev 15:24; 2 Sam 13:14). See Rashkow (1990:100-102) for a discussion of this verb form.

[4] Some modern commentators (e.g., Bright 1980:31; Holladay 1986:144-145) omit *shadûd* ("destroyed") for two reasons: first, it is not found in the Septuagint version where Jer 4:30 begins "And you, what are you doing," and second, it is a masculine predicate adjective, while the subject "you" is feminine. On the other hand, Thompson accepts its presence, translating it as "despoiled" (1980:231) as do most earlier commentators (see, e.g., Skinner 1940:37; Driver 1907:26; Streane 1805:43). The lack of gender agreement may be explained by noting that certain "inconsistencies in gender and even number are not uncommon in biblical Hebrew" (Barré 1986:614, 616). The Masoretic version of Jer 4:30 certainly contributes to the imagery of Israel as harlot.

[5] See Fewell and Gunn (1991a) and Niditch (1989) for recent discussions of the Jael-Sisera narrative.

[6] Cf. Cassuto (1975:71-102).

[7] Cross (1983), for example, sees images of Baal and El, gods who war against strong goddesses in the Baal-Anath tradition, reflected in the characterization of YHWH.

[8] Freud's position is that this statement is particularly significant in the development of female children. Chodorow (1978), however, claims mother-attachment is equally significant for boys.

[9] This point seems to have been made by Freud first in a footnote to Chapter VI of *Group Psychology and the Analysis of Ego* (1921c). He repeated it in Chapter XIII of the *Introductory Lectures on Psychoanalysis* (1916-1917) and in Chapter V of *Civilization and Its Discontents* (1930a). That exceptions may occur is shown by an example in the *New Introductory Lectures on Psychoanalysis*, where "the proud mother behaved otherwise; she withdrew her love from the child on account of his infirmity" (1916-17:530).

[10] As Eilberg-Schwartz argues, there is a strong connection between the theme of fertility and the practice of circumcision among various tribal peoples (1990:144-145).

[11] See, e.g., Graves and Patai (1983:240); Fox (1974:557-596); Sarna (1966:131-133); De Vaux (1961:46-48).

[12] Cf. Gen 46:8-27, which lists all the male descendants of Jacob through his wives and handmaids (Leah 33; Zilpah 16; Rachel 14; Bilhah 7). See also Exod 1:5, which states that "the total number of persons that were of Jacob's issue came to seventy, Joseph being already in Egypt." The discrepancy in the Gen 46 account is a result of the inclusion of Judah's sons Er and Onan, who died in Canaan, as well as Joseph and his two sons, Manasseh and Ephraim, who were already in Egypt. It appears that in Exod 1:5 (and in Deut 10:22 which repeats the same figure) "seventy" is a round number, used to evoke the idea of totality, comprehensiveness on a large scale, rather than literality. Another example of the rhetorical use of "seventy" is Genesis 10, where precisely seventy nations issue from the three sons of Noah, and these constitute the entire human family.

[13] Sarna (1970:170-71) states that the "thigh is symbolic of the reproductive organs, the seat of pro-creative powers" based on Genesis 24 (when Abraham wants his slave to fetch a wife for Isaac he commands the slave to "put your hand under my thigh and I will make you swear by the Lord . . . to go to my country, to my kindred to take a wife for my son") and Genesis 32 (when Jacob is finished fathering, he wrestles with an angel who touches the hollow of Jacob's thigh and puts it out of joint). In linguistic terms, however, this is incorrect; rather, it is an expression of a semantic universal that taboo body parts are subject to a spatial displacement by a more or less contiguous organ. As Vasvari (1990) discusses, the two legs above the knee, forming an angle which is the "lap," have been charged with genital meaning, the thighs connoted as the sex organ. In both Genesis examples, it is, therefore, the testicles which are being touched, the ultimate symbol (and reality) of male procreative powers.

[14] As Mace (1953:206) writes, "Abraham is the symbol of a change in a world view precipitated by the idea that men had come to view their role in conception as primary . . . the shift from the knowledge of participation to the assumption that it was the primary role."

[15] There are thirty-six instances of this formula in the Torah, all listed in *Mishnah Keritot* 1:1. This punishment is peculiar to ritual texts and is largely confined to offenses of a cultic and sexual nature. Since there is no biblical definition of *karat* ("cut off"), and in most texts, the impersonal, passive form of the verb is used (as here), not only the type of punishment but also the executive authority is uncertain.

[16] See also Steinmetz (1991) and Williams (1991).

[17] Boyarin (1992:476) posits that "circumcision is a male erasure of the female role in procreation."

[18] See, e.g., Sarna (1989:396-397); Cross (1983:4-43); Alt (1967); Haran (1965:51-52); Hyatt (1955).

[19] I have indicated Abraham's musings with italicized print and underlined the indeterminate pronouns.

[20] The Hebrew has, literally, "he/it was behind him/it," which is far from clear. It is likely that Abraham is standing just outside the door of the partially open tent, in a position to see Sarah and be overheard by her. This would explain why Abraham can address Sarah's whereabouts in answer to the visitors' question.

[21] There are numerous biblical uses of *tsahaq* in the *pi'el* verb form, and they are usually translated as "jest," "play," "make sport of," "toy with conjugal caresses," "make a toy of" (see, e.g., Gen 19:14; 21:9; 26:8; 39:14, 17; Exod 32:6; Judg 16:25). See also the noun *tsehoq* ("laughter"; "laughing-stock") (e.g., Gen 21:6; Ezek 23:32).

[22] Exactly who these visitors are is the subject of a great deal of theological debate. The Hebrew reads "*sheloshah 'anashîm*," literally "three men." According to the Ramban the visitors were angels who came to Abraham in the *form* of men—one to announce to Sarah that she would bear a son, one to heal Abraham, and one to overthrow Sodom. The Ramban then raises the question of whether angels partake of food, and resolves the issue by explaining that one course after the other "disappeared." That is, the angels really did not "eat."

[23] The Hebrew text presents a problem. The opening vocative is in the plural with a final long vowel. This is, however, also the form used for God. Rabbinic opinion is divided as to whether its use here is secular or sacred. Rashi and Ibn Ezra understand it to mean "My lords" (Shevu'ot 35b); Maimonides renders it "My Lord" (Yad, Yesodai Ha-Torah 6:9).

24 Cf. Benjamin (1979:239), who sees laughter as an action that "puts forth its own image and exists, absorbing and consuming it," thus establishing a kind of "dialectical justice"; see also Bakhtin (1968) who likewise understands laughter as a type of liberation.

25 *"Fehlleistungen,"* literally "faulty acts" or "faulty functions." The general concept did not exist before Freud, and the term "parapraxis" was invented for its translation into English by Strachey. The whole of *The Psychopathology of Everyday Life: Forgetting, Slips of the Tongue, Bungled Actions, Superstitions and Errors* (1901b:1-279) is devoted to a discussion of parapraxes, and Freud discusses them in many of his writings as the most suitable material for an introduction to his theories.

26 Lerner (1986) traces male control of female sexuality from its locus within the patriarchal family to regulation by the state.

27 Bal (1989a:216) argues that the newly married, childless-wife is in a precarious situation since she has not yet "proven herself" to be "worthy" of her new state. According to Bal, there is a "series" of nouns which indicate the "life-phase" of a young woman: *na'arah* ("young girl"—which Bal refers to as a phase of "near-ripeness"); *betûlah* ("virgin"); and *'almah* (the married woman given away by her father, before her first pregnancy, who can still be repudiated and, as such, is in a state of particular insecurity and danger).

28 A *serîs* need not necessarily be incapable of marital relations. Kugel (among others) notes that the term "eunuch" has a much broader range of meanings in Greek usage, and can mean someone stricken with infertility (1990:75-76). No understanding of the term is without problems, and it should be noted that while the Septuagint translates it to mean "eunuch," Targum Onkelos uses "officer." Kugel (1990:75) summarizes the issue succinctly: "Since Potiphar is generally identified by early exegetes with 'Potiphera' in Gen 41:45, the father of Aseneth, Joseph's future wife . . . how could a eunuch be the father of Aseneth? . . . Various ways around this apparent contradiction were found: Potiphar had become a eunuch only after Aseneth's birth; Potiphar was called Potiphera because he had been punished with castration (again, after Aseneth's birth); Aseneth was not Potiphar's real child; etc."

29 One theory of the derivation of the word *'almanah* ("widow") is that it stems from the verb *ne'elam* ("to be silenced").

30 As, of course, is Ruth. For a discussion of *'almanah* ("widow"), particularly as it applies to Ruth, see Rashkow (1990:140-141).

[31] See Fewell and Gunn (1991b); Rashkow (1990); and Sternberg for recent discussions of this narrative.

[32] Curiously, Simeon and Levi refer to Dinah in this verse as "our daughter" rather than "our sister." Perhaps it is because this verse is part of the negotiations which involve all of the "daughters" of Israel, Dinah included.

[33] Alternatively, Simeon's and Levi's response is directed against Jacob: "Will he [Jacob] treat our sister like a harlot?" According to Sternberg (1985:475), although the subject of the sentence seems to be Shechem, "he" is indeterminate for two reasons. First, Shechem has not been mentioned in the dialogue before. Second, this is the only place in Genesis 34 where the addressee is not specified. "Elsewhere he is identified by a direct or indirect object that immediately follows the reporting verb—even when his identity (as in verses 13-14) could be safely presupposed."

[34] Although *tsora'at* is often translated as "leprosy," it has none of the major symptoms of that malady (Preuss 1978; Sawyer 1976; Hulse 1975).

[35] For a discussion of the gradually increasing repression of female sexuality during the postexilic period, see Bullough (1976:74-75) and Epstein (1967:1-11).

[36] Terry Eagleton offers another word for phallogocentrism: "cocksureness" (1983:189)!

[37] On woman's sexuality "not so much as part of her feminine being but, rather, as an exclusive form of male experience," see Aschkenasy (1986:esp. 123-124).

[38] See esp. Cixous and Clément (1975); Moi (1981); Rose (1978); and the essays and further bibliography in Bernheimer and Kahane (1985).

BIBLIOGRAPHY

Alexander, Franz. 1948. *Fundamentals of Psychoanalysis*. New York: Norton.

Alt, A. 1967. "The God of the Fathers." In *Essays on Old Testament History and Religion*. Trans. R. A. Wilson. Garden City: Doubleday. Pp. 3-100.

Alter, Robert. 1991. "Biblical Imperatives and Literary Play." In *"Not in Heaven."* Rosenblatt and Sitterson, eds. Pp. 13-27.

——. 1990. "Sodom as Nexus: The Web of Design in Biblical Narrative." In *The Book and the Text*. R. Schwartz, ed. Pp. 146-160.

——. 1981. *The Art of Biblical Narrative*. New York: Basic.

Alter, Robert and Frank Kermode (eds.). 1987. *The Literary Guide to the Hebrew Bible*. Cambridge: Harvard Univ.

Andersen, F. I. 1974. *The Sentence in Biblical Hebrew*. The Hague: Mouton.

Archer, Leonie J. 1990. *Her Price Is Beyond Rubies: The Jewish Woman in Graeco-Roman Palestine*. Sheffield: JSOT.

——. 1987. "The Virgin and the Harlot in the Writings of Formative Judaism." *History Workshop: A Journal of Socialist and Feminist Historians* 24:1-16.

——. 1983. "The Role of Jewish Women in the Religion, Ritual and Cult of Graeco-Roman Palestine." In *Images of Women in Antiquity*. A. Cameron and A. Kuhrt, eds. Detroit: Wayne State Univ. Pp. 273-287.

Arlow, Jacob A. and Charles Brenner. 1964. "Psychoanalytic Concepts and the Structural Theory." *Journal of the American Psychoanalytic Association*. New York: International Universities.

Aschkenasy, Nehama. 1986. *Eve's Journey*. Philadelphia: Univ. of Pennsylvania.

Bach, Alice (ed.). 1990. *The Pleasure of Her Text: Feminist Readings of Biblical and Historical Texts*. Philadelphia: Trinity Press International.

——. 1990a. "The Pleasure of Her Text." In *The Pleasure of Her Text*. A. Bach, ed. Pp. 25-44.

Bakhtin, Mikhail. 1968. *Rabelais and His World*. H. Iswolsky, trans. Cambridge: MIT.

Bal, Mieke (ed.). 1989. *Anti-Covenant: Counter-Reading Women's Lives in the Hebrew Bible*. Sheffield: Almond.

——. 1989a. "Between Altar and Wondering Rock: Toward a Feminist Philology." In *Anti-Covenant*. M. Bal, ed. Pp. 211-231.

Balmary, Marie. 1979. *Psychoanalyzing Psychoanalysis: Freud and the Hidden Fault of the Father.* N. Lukacher, trans. Baltimore: Johns Hopkins Univ.

Bar-Efrat, Shimon. 1989. *Narrative Art in the Bible.* Sheffield: Almond.

Barré, Michael. 1986. "The Meaning of lᵓ ᵓšybnw in Amos 1:3-2:6." *JBL* 105:611-631.

Barricelli, Jean-Pierre and Joseph Gibaldi (eds.). 1982. *Interrelations of Literature.* New York: The Modern Language Association.

Bate, W. J. (ed.) *Criticism: The Major Texts.* 1970. New York: Harcourt Brace Jovanovich.

Bechtel, Lynn M. 1991. "Shame as a Sanction of Social Control in Biblical Israel: Judicial, Political, and Social Shaming." *JSOT* 49:47-76.

Benjamin, Walter. 1979. "Surrealism: The Last Snapshot of the European Intelligentsia." In *One-Way Street and Other Writings.* E. Jephcott and K. Shorter, trans. London: NLB.

Berlin, Adele. 1989. "Lexical Cohesion and Biblical Interpretation." *Hebrew Studies* 30:29-40.

———. 1983. *Poetics and Interpretation of Biblical Narrative.* Sheffield: Almond.

———. 1982. "On the Bible as Literature." *Prooftexts* 2:323-327.

Bernheimer, Charles and Claire Kahane (eds.). 1985. *In Dora's Case: Freud—Hysteria—Feminism.* New York: Columbia Univ.

Bigger, Stephen F. 1979. "The Family Laws of Leviticus 18 in Their Setting." *JBL* 98:187-293.

Bloom, Harold. 1976. "Poetic Crossing: Rhetoric and Psychology." *The Georgia Review* 30:495-526.

Boose, Lynda E. 1989. "The Father's House and the Daughter in It: The Structures of Western Culture's Daughter-Father Relationship." In *Daughters and Fathers.* L. E. Boose and B. S. Flowers, eds. Pp. 19-74.

Boose, Lynda E. and Betty S. Flowers (eds.). 1989. *Daughters and Fathers.* Baltimore: Johns Hopkins Univ.

Boswell, John. 1980. *Christianity, Social Tolerance, and Homosexuality.* Chicago: Univ. of Chicago.

Bottigheimer, Ruth B. 1987. *Grimms' Bad Girls and Bold Boys: The Moral and Social Vision of the Tales.* New Haven: Yale Univ.

Boyarin, Daniel. 1992. "'This We Know to Be the Carnal Israel': Circumcision and the Erotic Life of God and Israel." *Critical Inquiry* 18:474-505.

Bright, John. 1980. *Jeremiah.* Anchor Bible. Garden City: Doubleday.

Bullough, Vern. 1976. *Sexual Variance in Society and History.* Chicago and London: Univ. of Chicago.

Burney, C. F. 1970. *The Book of Judges.* New York: KTAV.

Cassuto, Umberto. 1978. *A Commentary on the Book of Genesis.* I. Abrahams, trans. Jerusalem: Magnes.

———. 1975. "The Israelite Epic." In *Biblical and Oriental Studies*. Vol. II. Jerusalem: Magnes.

Chodorow, Nancy. 1978. *The Reproduction of Mothering: Psychoanalysis and the Sociology of Gender*. Berkeley: Univ. of California.

Cixous, Hélène and Catherine Clément. 1975. *La jeune née*. Paris: UGE. (*The Newly Born Woman*. B. Wing, trans. Minneapolis: Univ. of Minnesota.)

Clines, David J. A. 1990. *What Does Eve Do to Help? and Other Readerly Questions to the Old Testament*. Sheffield: JSOT.

Cohen, Ralph (ed.). 1974. *New Directions in Literary History*. Baltimore: Johns Hopkins Univ.

Coogan, Michael D. 1978. *Stories from Ancient Canaan*. Philadelphia: Westminster.

Cross, Frank. 1983. *Canaanite Myth and Hebrew Epic: Essays in the History of the Religion of Israel*. Cambridge: Harvard Univ.

Culler, Jonathan. 1975. *Structuralist Poetics, Structuralism, Linguistics, and the Study of Literature*. Ithaca: Cornell Univ.

Culley, Robert C. 1976. *Studies in the Structure of Hebrew Narrative*. Philadelphia: Fortress.

Day, Peggy L. (ed.) 1989. *Gender and Difference In Ancient Israel*. Minneapolis: Fortress.

De Beauvoir, Simone. 1961. *The Second Sex*. H. M. Parshley, trans. New York: Bantam.

De Man, Paul. 1979. *Allegories of Reading: Figural Language in Rousseau, Nietszche, Rilke, and Proust*. New Haven: Yale Univ.

De Vaux, Roland O. 1961. *Ancient Israel: Its Life and Institutions*. New York: McGraw-Hill.

Douglas, Mary. 1966. *Purity and Danger: An Analysis of the Concepts of Pollution and Taboo*. New York: Praeger.

Driver, S. R. 1907. *The Book of the Prophet Jeremiah*. New York: Scribner.

Eagleton, Terry. 1983. *Literary Theory: An Introduction*. Minneapolis: Univ. of Minnesota.

Eilberg-Schwartz, Howard. 1990. *The Savage in Judaism: An Anthropology of Israelite Religion and Ancient Judaism*. Bloomington: Indiana Univ.

Epstein, Louis. 1967. *Sex Laws and Customs in Judaism*. New York: KTAV.

Exum, J. Cheryl and David J. A. Clines (eds.). 1993. *The New Literary Criticism and the Hebrew Bible*. Sheffield: JSOT.

Faur, José. 1986. *Golden Doves with Silver Dots: Semiotics and Textuality in Rabbinic Tradition*. Bloomington: Indiana Univ.

Felman, Shoshana (ed.). 1980. *Literature and Psychoanalysis: The Question of Reading: Otherwise*. Baltimore: Johns Hopkins Univ.

———. 1980a. "To Open the Question." In *Literature and Psychoanalysis*. S. Felman, ed. Pp. 5-10.

———. 1980b. "Turning the Screw of Interpretation." In *Literature and Psychoanalysis*. S. Felman, ed. Pp. 94-207.

Fewell, Danna Nolan (ed.). 1992. *Reading Between Texts*. Louisville: Westminster/John Knox.

Fewell, Danna Nolan and David M. Gunn. 1993. *Gender, Power, and Promise: The Subject of the Bible's First Story*. Nashville: Abingdon.

———. 1991a. "Controlling Perspectives: Women, Men, and the Authority of Violence in Judges 4 & 5." *JAAR* 58/3:389-411.

———. 1991b. "Tipping the Balance: Sternberg's Reader and the Rape of Dinah." *JBL* 110:193-212.

Fisch, Harold. 1984. *A Remembered Future: A Study in Literary Mythology*. Bloomington: Indiana Univ.

Fish, Stanley. 1980. *Is There a Text in This Class? The Authority of Interpretive Communities*. Cambridge: Harvard Univ.

———. 1980a. "Intepreting the *Variorum*." In *Reader-Response Criticism*. J. P. Tompkins, ed. Pp. 164-185.

Fishbane, Michael. 1991. " 'The Holy One Sits and Roars': Mythopoesis and the Midrashic Imagination." *Journal of Jewish Thought and Philosophy* 1:1-21.

———. 1985. *Biblical Interpretation in Ancient Israel*. Oxford: Clarendon.

Fokkelman, J. P. 1987. "Genesis." In *The Literary Guide to the Bible*. R. Alter and F. Kermode, eds. Pp. 36-55.

———. 1981. *Narrative Art and Poetry in the Books of Samuel*. Vol. I: King David (II Sam. 9-20 & I Kings 1-2). Studia Semitica Neerlandica 20. Assen: Van Gorcum.

Fox, Michael V. 1974. "The Sign of the Covenant: Circumcision in the Light of the Priestly 'ôt Etiologies." *Le Revue Biblique* 81:557-96.

Fox, Robin. 1967. *Kinship and Marriage: An Anthropological Perspective*. Cambridge: Cambridge Univ.

Freud, Sigmund. 1894a. "The Neuro-Psychoses of Defence." SE 3:43-86.

———. 1900a. *The Interpretation of Dreams*. SE 4:1-338 and 5:339-621.

———. 1901b. *The Psychopathology of Everyday Life: Forgetting, Slips of the Tongue, Bungled Actions, Superstitions and Errors*. SE 6:1-279.

———. 1905c. "Jokes as a Social Process." SE 8:140-58.

———. 1905d. *Three Essays on the Theory of Sexuality*. SE 7:135-243.

———. 1905e. "Fragment of an Analysis of a Case of Hysteria [Dora]." SE 7:7-122.

———. 1908e. "Creative Writers and Day-Dreaming." SE 9:143-156.

———. 1912b. "The Dynamics of Transference-Love." SE 12:99-158.

———. 1915a. "Observations on Transference-Love." SE 12:159-229.

———. 1915d. "Repression." SE 14:143-160.

———. 1916-17. *Introductory Lectures on Psycho-Analysis*. SE 15:15-239 and 16:243-463.

———. 1920g. *Beyond the Pleasure Principle*. SE 18:7-64.

———. 1921c. *Group Psychology and the Analysis of Ego*. SE 18:69-153.

———. 1923e. "The Infantile Genital Organization." SE 19:141-156.
———. 1925j. "Some Psychical Consequences of the Anatomical Distinction Between the Sexes." SE 19:241-260.
———. 1926e. The Question of Lay Analysis: Conversations with an Impartial Person. SE 12:183-250.
———. 1928b. "Dostoevsky and Patricide." SE 21:177-194.
———. 1930a. Civilization and Its Discontents. SE 21:64-145.
———. 1931b. "Female Sexuality." SE 21:223-245.
———. 1937c. "Analysis Terminable and Interminable." SE 23:216-253.
Freud, Sigmund and Joseph Breuer. 1895d. Studies on Hysteria. SE 2:3-305.
Frieden, Ken. 1990. Freud's Dream of Interpretation. Albany: SUNY.
Friedman, Richard (ed.). 1983. The Poet and the Historian: Essays in Literary and Historical Biblical Criticism. Chico, CA: Scholars.
Froula, Christine. 1989. "The Daughter's Seduction: Sexual Violence and Literary History." In Daughters and Fathers. L. E. Boose and B. S. Flowers, eds. Pp. 111-135.
———. 1983. "When Eve Reads Milton: Undoing the Canonical Economy." Critical Inquiry 10:321-348.
Frye, Northrop. 1982. The Great Code: The Bible and Literature. New York: Harcourt.
Gallop, Jane. 1989. "The Father's Seduction." In Daughter and Fathers. L. E. Boose and B. S. Flowers, eds. Pp. 97-110.
Gesenius, W. 1909. Rev. 1910. Hebrew Grammar. E. Kautzsch, ed. Oxford: Oxford Univ.
Girard, René. 1986. The Scapegoat. Baltimore: Johns Hopkins Univ.
Good, Edwin M. 1981. Irony in the Old Testament. Sheffield: Almond.
Good, Robert M. 1982. "Metaphorical Gleanings from Ugarit." Journal of Jewish Studies 33:55-59.
Graves, Robert and Raphael Patai. 1983. Hebrew Myths: The Book of Genesis. New York: Greenwich House.
Grube, G. M. A. (trans. of Aristotle). 1958. On Poetry and Style. Indianapolis: Bobbs-Merrill.
Gunkel, Hermann. 1966. Legends of Genesis. New York: Schocken.
Gunn, David. 1980. The Fate of King Saul: An Interpretation of a Biblical Story. Sheffield: JSOT.
———. 1974. "Narrative Patterns and Oral Tradition in Judges and Samuel." VT 24:286-317.
Gunn, David M. and Danna Nolan Fewell. 1993. Narrative in the Hebrew Bible. Oxford: Oxford Univ.
Halpern, Baruch. 1983. "Doctrine by Misadventure: Between the Israelite Source and the Biblical Historian." In The Poet and the Historian. R. Friedman, ed. Pp. 41-74.
Handelman, Susan. 1982. The Slayers of Moses. Albany: SUNY.
Haran, M. 1965. "The Religion of the Patriarchs." Annual of the Swedish Theological Institute 4:51-52.

Harris, R. 1976. "Woman in the Ancient Near East." In *IDBSupp*. Nashville: Abingdon.

Hartman, Geoffrey (ed.). 1978. *Psychoanalysis and the Question of the Text*. Baltimore: Johns Hopkins Univ.

———. 1975. *The Fate of Reading and Other Essays*. Chicago: Univ. of Chicago.

Hartman, Geoffrey and Sanford Budick (eds.). 1986. *Midrash and Literature*. New Haven: Yale Univ.

Heine, Susanne. 1989. *Matriarchs, Goddesses, and Images of God: A Critique of Feminist Theology*. J. Bowden, trans. Minneapolis: Augsburg.

Herman, Judith Lew and Lisa Hirschman. 1981. *Father-Daughter Incest*. Cambridge: Harvard Univ.

Heschel, Susannah (ed.). 1983. *On Being a Jewish Feminist: A Reader*. New York: Schocken.

Holladay, William. 1986. *Jeremiah 1: A Commentary on the Book of the Prophet Jeremiah*. Hermeneia. Philadelphia: Fortress.

Holland, Norman. 1975. *5 Readers Reading*. New Haven: Yale Univ.

———. 1964. *Psychoanalysis and Shakespeare*. New York: McGraw-Hill.

Holtz, Barry W. (ed.) 1984. *Back to the Sources: Reading the Classic Jewish Texts*. New York: Summit.

Horner, Tom. 1978. *Jonathan Loved David: Homosexuality in Biblical Times*. Philadelphia: Westminster.

Horney, Karen. 1950. *Neurosis and Human Growth*. New York: Norton.

Hulse, E. V. 1975. "The Nature of Biblical 'Leprosy' and the Use of Alternative Medical Terms in Modern Translations of the Bible." *Palestine Exploration Quarterly* 107:87-105.

Hyatt, J. P. 1955. "Yahweh as the God of My Father." *VT* 5:130-136.

Irigaray, Luce. 1977. *Ce Sexe qui n'en est pas un*. Paris: Minuit. (*This Sex Which Is Not One*. C. Porter and C. Burke, trans. Ithaca: Cornell Univ.)

Iser, Wolfgang. 1978. *The Act of Reading: A Theory of Aesthetic Response*. Baltimore: Johns Hopkins Univ.

———. 1974. "The Reading Process: A Phenomenological Approach." In *New Directions in Literary History*. R. Cohen, ed. Pp.125-147.

Jakobson, Roman and Morris Halle. 1975. *Fundamentals of Language*. 2nd edn. The Hague: Mouton.

Jameson, Fredric. 1977. "Imaginary and Symbolic in Lacan: Marxism, Psychoanalytic Criticism, and the Problem of the Subject." *Yale French Studies* 55/56:338-395.

Jeansonne, Sharon Pace. 1990. *The Women of Genesis: From Sarah to Potiphar's Wife*. Minneapolis: Fortress.

Jobling, David. 1986. *The Sense of Biblical Narrative II*. Sheffield: JSOT.

Jones, Ernest. 1949. *Hamlet and Oedipus*. London: Victor Gollancz.

———. 1948. "The Death of Hamlet's Father." *International Journal of Psychoanalysis 29.*

———. 1927. "The Early Development of Female Sexuality." *International Journal of Psychoanalysis 8.*

Keil, C. F. and F. Delitzsch. 1971. *Commentary on the Old Testament in Ten Volumes. Vol. 1: The First Book of Moses (Genesis).* Grand Rapids: Eerdmans.

Koch, Klaus. 1969. *The Growth of the Biblical Tradition.* New York: Scribner.

Kristeva, Julia. 1971. *Séméiotiké: Recherches pour une sémiologique.* Paris: Seuil.

Kugel, James L. 1990. *In Potiphar's House: The Interpretive Life of Biblical Texts.* San Francisco: Harper Collins.

———. 1982. "On the Bible as Literature." *Prooftexts* 2:328-332.

———. 1981. "On the Bible and Literary Criticism." *Prooftexts* 1:217-236.

Kurzweil, Edith and William Phillips (eds.). 1983. *Literature and Psychoanalysis.* New York: Columbia Univ.

Labushagne, C. J. 1974. "The *nasû-nadãnu* Formula and Its Biblical Equivalent." In *Travels in the World of the Old Testament: Studies Presented to M. A. Beek.* M. S. H. G. Heerma van Voss et al, eds. Assen: Van Gorcum.

Lacan, Jacques. 1982. *Feminine Sexuality.* J. Mitchell and Jacqueline Rose, trans. J. Rose, ed. New York: Norton.

———. 1977. *The Four Fundamental Concepts of Psycho-Analysis.* London: Tavistock.

———. 1968. *Speech and Language in Psychoanalysis.* A. Wilden, trans. Baltimore: Johns Hopkins Univ.

———. 1958. "Les Formations de l'inconscient." *Bulletin de Psychologie* 12/4:250-256.

Laing, R. D. 1974. *Knots.* Harmondsworth: Penguin.

Landy, Francis. 1983. *Paradoxes of Paradise: Identity and Difference in the Song of Songs.* Sheffield: Almond.

Lang, Bernhard. 1983. *Monotheism and the Prophetic Minority: An Essay in Biblical History and Sociology.* Sheffield: Almond.

Laplanche, Jean and J. B. Pontalis. 1968. "Fantasy and the Origins of Sexuality." *International Journal of Psychoanalysis* 49:1-18.

Lattimore, Richmond. (trans. of Aeschylus). 1967. "The Eumenides." *Oresteia.* Part 3. Chicago: Univ. of Chicago.

Leach, Edmund. 1983. *Culture and Communication: The Logic by Which Symbols Are Connected.* Cambridge: Cambridge Univ.

Leibowitz, Nehama. 1981. *Studies in Bereshit (Genesis): In the Context of Ancient and Modern Jewish Bible Commentary.* A. Newman, trans. Jerusalem: World Zionist Organization.

Lerner, Gerda. 1986. *The Creation of Patriarchy.* New York: Oxford Univ.

Loewenstein, Rudolph M. 1957. "Some Thoughts on Interpretation in the Theory and Practice of Psychoanalysis." *Psychoanalytic Study of the Child* 12.

Lord, Albert B. 1968. *The Singer of Tales*. New York: Atheneum.

Mace, David. 1953. *Hebrew Marriage: A Sociological Study*. New York: Philosophical Library.

Malina, Bruce. 1985. "Hospitality." In *Harper's Bible Dictionary*. P. J. Achtemeier, ed. San Francisco: Harper & Row. Pp. 408-409.

Maly, E. 1956. "Genesis 12, 10-20; 20, 1-18; 26, 7-11 and the Pentateuchal Question." *CBQ* 18:255-262.

Masson, Jeffrey Moussaieff. 1983. *The Assault on Truth: Freud's Suppression of the Seduction Theory*. New York: Farrar.

McClelland, David C. 1964. *The Roots of Consciousness*. Princeton: Van Nostrand.

McKnight, Edgar V. 1988. *Post-Modern Use of the Bible: The Emergence of Reader-Oriented Criticism*. Nashville: Abingdon.

Miller, Alice. 1984. *Thou Shalt Not Be Aware: Society's Betrayal of the Child*. H. Hannum and H. Hannum, trans. New York: Farrar, Straus, and Giroux.

Miscall, Peter D. 1983. *The Workings of Old Testament Narrative*. Philadelphia: Fortress.

———. 1979. "Literary Unity in Old Testament Narrative." *Semeia* 15:27-44.

Mitchell, Juliet. 1975. *Psychoanalysis and Feminism*. New York: Random House.

Moi, Toril. 1981. "Representation of Patriarchy: Sexuality and Epistemology in Freud's Dora." *Feminist Review* 9:60-74.

Moore, George F. 1976. *A Critical and Exegetical Commentary on Judges*. Edinburgh: T & T Clark.

Moss, Donald. 1989. "On Situating the Object: Thoughts on the Maternal Function, Modernism and Post-Modernism." *American Imago* 46/4:353-369.

Newsom, Carol A. and Sharon H. Ringe (eds.). 1992. *The Women's Bible Commentary*. Louisville: Westminster/John Knox.

Niditch, Susan. 1989. "Eroticism and Death in the Tale of Jael." In *Gender and Difference in Ancient Israel*. P. L. Day, ed. Pp. 43-57.

———. 1987. *Underdogs and Tricksters: A Prelude to Biblical Folklore*. San Francisco: Harper.

———. 1982. "The 'Sodomite' Theme in Judges 19-20: Family, Community, and Social Disintegration." *CBQ* 44:365-378.

———. 1980. *The Symbolic Vision in Biblical Tradition*. Chico, CA: Scholars.

Ochshorn, Judith. 1981. *The Female Experience and the Nature of the Divine*. Bloomington: Indiana Univ.

Oppenheim, A. Leo. 1956. "The Interpretation of Dreams in the Ancient Near East." *Transactions of the American Philosophical Association* 46/3.

Ozick, Cynthia. 1983. "Notes Toward Finding the Right Question." In *On Being a Jewish Feminist*. S. Heschel, ed. Pp. 120-151.

Piers, G. and M. Singer. 1953. *Shame and Guilt*. New York: Norton.

Pitt-Rivers, Julian. 1977. *The Fate of Shechem*. Cambridge Studies in Social Anthropology Series. Cambridge: Cambridge Univ.

Plaskow, Judith. 1990. *Standing Again at Sinai: Judaism from a Feminist Perspective*. San Francisco: Harper & Row.

Poland, Lynn. 1990. "The Bible and the Rhetorical Sublime." In *The Bible as Rhetoric*. M. Warner, ed. Pp. 29-50.

Polzin, Robert. 1975. " 'The Ancestress of Israel in Danger' in Danger." *Semeia* 3:81-98.

Pope, Marvin. 1977. *Song of Songs*. Garden City, New York: Doubleday.

Preuss, J. 1978. *Biblical and Talmudic Medicine*. F. Rosner, ed. and trans. New York: Sanhedrin.

Ragland-Sullivan, Ellie. 1986. *Jacques Lacan and the Philosophy of Psychoanalysis*. Urbana: Univ. of Illinois.

Rashkow, Ilona N. 1990. *Upon the Dark Places: Anti-Semitism and Sexism in English Renaissance Biblical Translation*. Sheffield: Almond.

Reiter, Rayna (ed.). 1975. *Toward an Anthropology of Women*. New York: Monthly Review.

Resch, Andreas. 1964. *Der Traum in Heilsplan Gottes: Deutung und Bedeutung des Traums im Alten Testament*. Freiburg: Herder.

Ricoeur, Paul. 1970. *Freud and Philosophy: An Essay on Interpretation*. D. Savage, trans. New Haven: Yale Univ.

Riffaterre, Michael. 1978. *The Semiotics of Poetry*. Bloomington: Indiana Univ.

Rimmon-Kenan, Shlomith. 1983. *Narrative Fiction: Contemporary Poetics*. London: Methuen.

Rodes, A. B. 1977. "Israel's Prophets as Intercessors." In *Scripture in History and Theology*. A. L. Meril and T. W. Overholt, eds. Pittsburgh: Pickwick.

Rose, Jacqueline. 1982. "Introduction." In Jacques Lacan, *Feminine Sexuality*. Pp. 27-57.

———. 1978. "'Dora'—fragment of an analysis." *m/f* 2:5-21.

Rosenberg, Joel. 1986. *King and Kin: Political Allegory in the Hebrew Bible*. Bloomington: Indiana Univ.

———. 1984. "Biblical Narrative." In *Back to the Sources*. B. W. Holtz, ed. Pp. 31-82.

Rosenblatt, Jason P. and Joseph C. Sitterson, Jr. (eds.) 1991. *"Not in Heaven": Coherence and Complexity in Biblical Narrative*. Bloomington: Indiana Univ.

Rosenblatt, Louise. 1938. *Literature as Exploration*. London: Heinemann.

Rowe, Karen E. 1979. "Feminism and Fairy Tales." *Women's Studies* 6:15-47.

Rubin, Gayle. 1975. "The Traffic in Women: Notes on the 'Political Economy' of Sex." In *Toward an Anthropology of Women*. R. Reiter, ed. Pp. 157-210.

Rush, Florence. 1980. *The Best-Kept Secret: Sexual Abuse of Children*. Englewood Cliffs: Prentice-Hall.

Russell, Letty M. (ed.) 1985. *Feminist Interpretation of the Bible*. Philadelphia: Westminster.

Sandmel, Samuel. 1961. "The Haggadah Within Scripture." *JBL* 80:105-122.

Sarna, Nahum. 1989. *Genesis*. Philadelphia: The Jewish Publication Society.

———. 1970. *Understanding Genesis: The Heritage of Biblical Israel*. New York: Shocken.

———. 1966. *Understanding Genesis*. New York: McGraw-Hill.

Sawyer, J. F. A. "A Note on the Etymology of Sārat." *VT* 26:241-245.

Schur, Max. 1972. *Freud: Living and Dying*. New York: International Universities.

Schwartz, Murray M. and David Willbern. 1982. "Literature and Psychology." In *Interrelations of Literature*. J.-P. Barricelli and J. Gibaldi, eds. Pp. 205-224.

Schwartz, Regina (ed.). 1990. *The Book and the Text: The Bible and Literary Theory*. Oxford: Basil Blackwell.

———. 1990a. "Joseph's Bones and the Resurrection of the Text: Remembering the Bible." In *The Book and the Text*. Pp. 40-59.

Setel, T. Drorah. 1985. "Prophets and Pornography: Female Sexual Imagery in Hosea." In *Feminist Interpretation of the Bible*. L. M. Russell, ed. Pp. 86-95.

Shelley, Percy Bysshe. 1821. "A Defense of Poetry." In *Criticism: Major Texts*. W. J. Bate, ed. Pp. 429-435.

Skinner, John. 1940. *Prophecy and Religion: Studies in the Life of Jeremiah*. Cambridge: Cambridge Univ.

———. 1930. *A Critical and Exegetical Commentary on Genesis*. 2nd edn. Edinburgh: T & T Clark.

Skura, Meredith Anne. 1981. *The Literary Use of the Psychoanalytic Process*. New Haven: Yale Univ.

Slatoff, Walter. 1970. *With Respect to Readers: Dimensions of Literary Response*. Ithaca: Cornell Univ.

Smith, Joseph H. 1986. "Primitive Guilt." In *Pragmatism's Freud*. J. H. Smith and W. Kerrigan, eds. Pp. 52-78.

Smith, Joseph H. and William Kerrigan (eds.). 1986. *Pragmatism's Freud: The Moral Disposition of Psychoanalysis*. Baltimore: Johns Hopkins Univ.

Soggin, Alberto. 1981. *Judges*. Philadelphia: Westminster.

Speiser, E. A. 1964. *Genesis*. Garden City, N.Y.: Doubleday.

Steinmetz, Devora. 1991. *From Father to Son: Kinship, Conflict, and Continuity in Genesis*. Louisville: Westminster/John Knox.

Steinsaltz, Adin. 1984. *Biblical Images: Men and Women of the Book.* Y. Hanegbi and Y. Keshet, trans. New York: Basic.

Sternberg, Meir. 1985. *The Poetics of Biblical Narrative: Ideological Literature and the Drama of Reading.* Bloomington: Indiana Univ.

Stone, Merlin. 1976. *When God Was a Woman.* New York: Dial.

Streane, A. W. 1805. *The Book of the Prophet Jeremiah, Together with Lamentations.* Cambridge: Cambridge Univ.

Teubal, Savina J. 1990. *Hagar the Egyptian: The Lost Tradition of the Matriarchs.* San Francisco: Harper & Row.

Thompson, J. A. 1980. *The Book of Jeremiah.* Grand Rapids: Eerdmans.

Tompkins, Jane P. (ed.) 1980. *Reader-Response Criticism: From Formalism to Post-Structuralism.* Baltimore: Johns Hopkins Univ.

———. 1980a. "An Introduction to Reader-Response Criticism." In *Reader-Response Criticism.* Pp. ix-xxvi.

Trible, Phyllis. 1984. *Texts of Terror: Literary-Feminist Readings of Biblical Narratives.* Philadelphia: Fortress.

———. 1978. *God and the Rhetoric of Sexuality.* Philadelphia: Fortress.

Van Seters, John. 1975. *Abraham in History and Tradition.* New Haven: Yale Univ.

Vasvari, Louise O. 1990. "A Tale of 'Tailing' in the *Libro De Buen Amor.*" *Journal of Interdisciplinary Literary Studies* 2/1:13-41.

Vawter, Bruce. 1977. *On Genesis: A New Reading.* Garden City: Doubleday.

Vermeule, Emily. 1979. *Aspects of Death in Early Greek Art and Poetry.* Sather Classical Lecture Series 46. Berkeley: Univ. of California.

Warner, Martin (ed.). 1990. *The Bible as Rhetoric: Studies in Biblical Persuasion and Credibility.* London: Routledge.

Weber, Samuel. 1982. *The Legend of Freud.* Minneapolis: Univ. of Minnesota.

Wegner, Judith Romney. 1992. "Leviticus." In *The Women's Bible Commentary.* C. A. Newsom and S. H. Ringe, eds. Pp. 363-344.

Weinfield, Moshe. 1985. "Sarah and Abimelech (Genesis 20) Against the Background of an Assyrian Law and the Genesis Apocryphon." *Festschrift Delcore. Alter Orient und Altes Testament* 215:431-435.

Willbern, David. 1989. "*Filia Oedipi*: Father and Daughter in Freudian Theory." In *Daughters and Fathers.* L. E. Boose and B. S. Flowers, eds. Pp. 75-96.

Williams, James G. 1991. *The Bible, Violence and the Sacred.* New York: Harper Collins.

———. 1980. "The Beautiful and the Barren: Conventions in Biblical Type-Scenes." *JSOT* 17:107-119.

Winnicott, D. W. 1971. "Mirror-Role of Mother and Family in Child Development." In *Playing and Reality.* London: Tavistock. Pp. 111-118.

Wolfson, F. 1987. "Circumcision, Vision of God, and Textual Interpretation: From Midrashic Trope to Mystical Symbol." *History of Religions* 27:189-215.

Wright, Elizabeth. 1984. *Psychoanalytic Criticism: Theory in Practice*. London: Methuen.

ABBREVIATIONS

CBQ	*Catholic Biblical Quarterly*
IDBSupp.	*Interpreter's Dictionary of the Bible Supplement*
JAAR	*Journal of the American Academy of Religion*
JBL	*Journal of Biblical Literature*
JSOT	*Journal for the Study of the Old Testament*
VT	*Vetus Testamentum*

The abbreviation SE designates *The Standard Edition of the Complete Psychological Works of Sigmund Freud*, edited and translated by James Strachey, 24 vols. (London: The Hogarth Press and The Institute of Psycho-Analysis, 1953-74). Individual works from the SE cited in the text are listed chronologically, by the year of the first German edition.

INDEXES

AUTHORS

116, 123, 124, 128
Halle, Morris 119
Halpern, Baruch 34
Handelman, Susan 117
Haran, M. 126
Harris, R. 88
Hartman, Geoffrey 115, 117
Heine, Susanne 95
Herman, Judith 71, 73, 121
Hirschman, Lisa 71, 73, 121
Holladay, William 124
Holland, Norman 18-19, 57,
63, 120
Horner, Tom 123
Horney, Karen 69, 73
Hulse, E. V. 128
Hyatt, J. P. 126
Irigaray, Luce 79, 124
Iser, Wolfgang 21, 27, 86, 124
Jakobson, Roman 119
Jameson, Fredric 122-123
Jeansonne, Sharon Pace 117
Jobling, David 93
Jones, Ernest 17-18, 108,
115-116
Kahane, Claire 128
Keil, C. F. 42
Koch, Klaus 29, 33
Kristeva, Julia 36
Kugel, James L. 117, 127
Kurzweil, Edith 115
Labushagne, C. J. 120
Lacan, Jacques 36-39, 55,
58, 94, 106, 123
Laing, R. D. 26
Landy, Francis 87, 120
Lang, Bernhard 88
Laplanche, Jean 122
Lattimore, Richmond 92
Leach, Edmund 103
Leibowitz, Nehama 82-83
Lerner, Gerda 82, 123, 127
Lévi-Strauss, Claude 68
Loewenstein, Rudolph M. 23
Lord, Albert B. 30
Mace, David 92, 126

Malina, Bruce 123
Maly, E. 29
Masson, Jeffrey M. 73
McKnight, Edgar V. 16, 116
McClelland, David C. 86
Miller, Alice 121
Miscall, Peter D. 42, 96,
117, 118
Mitchell, Juliet 108, 124
Moi, Toril 128
Moss, Donald 53-54
Niditch, Susan 30, 31-32, 55,
61, 83, 87, 118, 119,
123, 124
Ochshorn, Judith 88
Oppenheim, A. Leo 119
Patai, Raphael 124
Phillips, William 115
Piers, G. 69
Pitt-Rivers, Julian 68
Plaskow, Judith 88, 95, 102
Polzin, Robert 33, 117
Poland, Lynn 38
Pontalis, J. B. 122
Pope, Marvin 87
Pruess, J. 128
Ragland-Sullivan, E. 122
Rashkow, Ilona N. 67, 124,
127
Resch, Andreas 60
Ricoeur, Paul 117
Riffaterre, Michael 21, 48
Rimmon-Kenan, Shlomith 116
Rodes, A. B. 120
Rose, Jacqueline 122, 128
Rosenblatt, Louise 19-20
Rosenburg, Joel 28-30, 31, 35
Rowe, Karen E. 102
Rubin, Gayle 79, 121
Rush, Florence 122
Sandmel, Samuel 33
Sarna, Nahum 32, 63, 82,
98, 99, 123, 125
Sawyer, J. F. A. 128
Schur, Max 75
Schwartz, Murray M. 19

BIBLICAL REFERENCES